Punishment-Free Parenting

"Jon Fogel's *Punishment-Free Parenting* is a refreshing invitation to millennial parents to reimagine how we raise our children. With profound empathy and insight, Fogel challenges us to step away from unhelpful punitive models and instead embrace the path of conscious, mindful discipline. His approach is both practical and deeply transformative, empowering parents to nurture cooperation and trust without fear or shame. A powerful guide for those on the journey to awaken themselves to a better way to parent."

—Dr. Shefali, *New York Times* bestselling author of *The Conscious Parent*

"Every parent needs this book. The fresh approach to parenting is a lifesaver!"

—Vanessa Van Edwards, bestselling author of *Cues*

"*Punishment-Free Parenting* is a research-based book rich with storytelling and effective examples. It's an absolute must-read written by the perfect expert for everyone in a caregiving relationship who strives for true connection while breaking generational cycles."

—Eve Rodsky, *New York Times* bestselling author of *Fair Play* and *Find Your Unicorn Space*

Punishment-Free
PARENTING

Punishment-Free PARENTING

The Brain-Based Way to Raise
Kids Without Raising Your Voice

JON FOGEL

CONVERGENT

New York

Published in the United States by Convergent Books, an imprint of Random House, a division of Penguin Random House LLC, New York.

CONVERGENT BOOKS is a registered trademark and the Convergent colophon is a trademark of Penguin Random House LLC.

LIBRARY OF CONGRESS CATALOGING-IN-PUBLICATION DATA
Names: Fogel, Jon, author.
Title: Punishment-free parenting / by Jon Fogel.
Description: First edition. | New York, NY: Convergent, 2025 |
Includes bibliographical references and index.
Identifiers: LCCN 2024019980 (print) | LCCN 2024019981 (ebook) |
ISBN 9780593735466 (hardcover) | ISBN 9780593735473 (ebook)
Subjects: LCSH: Discipline of children. | Child rearing. | Parenting.
Classification: LCC HQ770.4 .F64 2025 (print) | LCC HQ770.4 (ebook) |
DDC 649/.64—dc23/eng/20240522
LC record available at https://lccn.loc.gov/2024019980
LC ebook record available at https://lccn.loc.gov/2024019981

Printed in the United States of America on acid-free paper

convergentbooks.com

4 6 8 9 7 5 3

Book design by Jo Anne Metsch

*This book is dedicated to the woman
who truly inspires me in all aspects of my life but
especially as a dad. Jess, it's you and me against
the world and I could not imagine a better
partner to go into battle with.*

Foreword

Fifteen years ago, Dan Siegel and I began writing out the ideas that would soon become *The Whole Brain Child*. That book presented a host of ideas that, for many, felt completely new, even revolutionary. Now I feel incredibly grateful that, to a huge extent, many of those concepts have entered mainstream thought and been accepted as essential, even fundamental, in terms of how many of us look at parent-child relationships.

I love when a new book or one of the parenting accounts I follow on social media refers to "the upstairs and downstairs brain" without even having to explain the phrase. Or when they mention how important it is to connect before we redirect. The concepts that behavior is communication and that discipline is about teaching rather than punishment felt almost groundbreaking when we first started writing our books. Now those concepts are often treated as givens by a whole new generation of parenting experts and teachers. I really love that.

And still, there's plenty of work to be done when it comes to how discipline is generally viewed and practiced. We can use the wear-worn metaphor of the pendulum.

It's crucial that we continue to evolve beyond the old-school "I'll give you something to cry about" kind of reactive discipline: the one where discipline is seen strictly as punishment, almost retribution, that parents mete out when children disobey, never thinking about the cost of that punishment on the parent-child relationship (or on the child). That's one extreme of the pendulum's arc, and it's good that so many parents have now swung away from it.

That said, though, at times I'm uncomfortable with how far things have swung the other way. A mom recently asked me what she should do when her three-year-old won't put on his shoes before school. She said that she'd spent twenty minutes in an empathic, reflective dialogue with her preschooler, and he still refused. That this mom didn't realize there's a time to (lovingly and respectfully) scoop up her child and his shoes while walking to the minivan so he won't miss school is evidence that the pendulum has built up a head of steam and veered right past healthy discipline.

My guess is that this mother has been influenced by a school of thought often referred to as "gentle parenting," which my books sometimes get lumped in with. At times people even say that Dan and I helped cultivate that movement. And while emotional attunement is the hallmark of a healthy parent-child relationship—I always say to keep the relationship on the front burner and to keep everything else, aside from safety, on the back burner—the issue I have with some (but not all) so-called "gentle parenting" approaches is that they often come without the structure and limits kids need. The research is very clear: It's important that children have an adult in their lives who's in charge, who's willing to set boundaries and say no, and who teaches them what's acceptable and what's not as they navigate their world. In other words, gentleness, respectful communication, and emotional responsiveness are crucial, but they shouldn't come at the expense of the limits kids need to feel safe and to practice putting on the brakes as they grow and develop. And yes, it's sometimes even *good* for our kids when we pick them up and head for the car while empathetically saying something like, "I can see that you don't want to put your shoes on. And we are getting in the car now. It's OK to feel mad and sad that we're leaving, and I'm right here with you while you're having a hard time."

It's the other side of the pendulum that concerns me more, though. There's where we *really* have work to do. The world is full of parents who still see discipline as a practice that relies on control and power and pain. Too often, they think of discipline moments as times to punish, to make kids feel shame, and to use punitive approaches that don't do much to help children build skills or learn to self-discipline. Granted, this punitive approach to misbehavior can sometimes lead to compliance in the moment. But often it results only in kids getting better at *hiding* their misbehavior to avoid the consequences, thus breaking down parent-child trust and communication. Studies clearly demonstrate that when it comes to making it more likely that children will behave better in the future, the punitive method lags far behind the more relational one.

At its foundation, discipline is about teaching so that kids can continue to develop the skills and capacities to help them behave better both now and in the future. For almost seventy years, the research has consistently shown that the best way to do that is to *combine* nurture and structure, emotional responsiveness and boundaries. Doing so works from a relationship-based, teaching-centric approach in which children feel cared for *and also* understand the way the world really works. When we parent with these dual goals in mind, we move toward the ultimate objective of effective discipline: kids learning to be *self*-disciplined as they move toward and into adolescence and adulthood.

That's where my colleague and friend Jon Fogel comes in. If you're one of the hundreds of thousands of people who follow his work on a regular basis, then you know how much he believes in and teaches the fundamental concept that children need us to set boundaries and limits in a way that respects them, honors their emotional lives, and prioritizes our relationships with them. You also know that he has a remarkable gift for taking important and sometimes complicated concepts and making them clear and accessible. And he does it in such a fun way! Reading his work, you'll feel like you're hanging out with an entertaining, smart friend whose quirk is that he just happens to know a lot about brains and effective parenting.

You'll also find that his work isn't shaming—in fact, it's downright encouraging. As you read along, notice how you feel supported as Jon teaches you; how he's in it with you. Some parents avoid doing self-work and reading parenting books because they're afraid of feeling inadequate or judged. But Jon goes to great lengths to make sure you know that *punishing yourself* for not being the perfect parent is just as ineffective as punishing your kids. The way he communicates lets you know that he's like the rest of us—human. Like you (and like me), he has also experienced the struggles and made the mistakes that come with being a parent.

On top of all this, Jon is an actively engaged dad. Watch his compelling online videos or have a conversation with him and you'll immediately pick up on the same thing you'll see in the following pages: He's a dad first—one who also happens to be a well-respected parenting voice. His enthusiasm and vulnerable honesty make the book a treasure trove for people who have been wanting a research-backed parenting book to give to the parents in their lives—even, and especially, the ones who wouldn't typically read parenting books.

Punishment-Free Parenting is the practical science-grounded guide for how to discipline our children in ways that promote relationships, build skills, create a felt sense of safety, and eventually lead to self-discipline. Most caregivers find discipline one of the least pleasant parts of parenting. Most parents don't want to punish their kids. They do it because they either don't know another way, or they get really reactive in the moment, or they're afraid that if they don't, then their kids won't turn out to be great people. Jon will serve as your guide, coaching you through each of these reasons why parents turn to punishment, and then helping you discipline effectively *without* punishment. And along the way, you'll feel like the book is a great big hug that reminds you that we're all in this together and that we're better parents than we think we are.

As you embark on this journey with Jon Fogel, I encourage you to approach it with an open heart and mind. The ideas presented here may challenge some long-held beliefs, but they also offer the promise of a more fulfilling relationship with your kids and more effective ways of guiding behavior while you cultivate your children's developing brains. Whether you're a parent, grandparent, educator, clinician, or some other leader, I'm confident you'll find valuable insights in these pages. And I'm thrilled that this book will add to the collection of books by tremendous thinkers and leaders who help us raise children who are happy, healthy, and fully themselves.

TINA PAYNE BRYSON, PhD
Co-author of *The Whole-Brain Child*,
No Drama-Discipline, The Yes Brain,
The Power of Showing Up, and *The Way of Play*
Author of *The Bottom-Line for Baby*

Contents

Introduction

I was not always a punishment-free parent. I remember a time when I left my oldest son to cry in a dark room because I was so upset I couldn't look at him. He couldn't have been two years old.

I remember the first time I wanted to grab him and throw him to the ground for hitting me in the face with one of his toys. I felt the rage course through my body like poison as I looked down and, inexplicably, felt the urge to *hurt* the person in my life I loved the most.

I've lost track of the number of times I've raised my voice at my kids; when I close my eyes I can clearly picture their terrified faces those times when my temper boiled over and I snapped.

Then there are the times when I chose to leverage *punishments* when I was calm. When I took away a prized toy, or threatened to give them a time-out if they wouldn't stop whining. These times I was motivated by a total certainty that punishments and threats of punishment were the only effective ways to *teach kids a lesson.*

But I also remember being a child. I remember those times when my parents trapped me in a dark room when I was in grade school. I remember crying through the door that if they would just open it so I could know they were there, I promised I would be good next time. I remember that fear so vividly and, in spite of that, I did it to my own son.

There were also those times I would stare at cookbooks as I sat on our tiny time-out chair, wondering when I might be allowed to leave.

To their credit, my parents never hit me when I was young, even though the same cannot be said of their childhood experiences. But there were times my dad would get home, stressed out from twelve hours at work, and yell or ground me for the house being messy. Sometimes my parents would take away something I liked or something I liked to do just to teach me a lesson. They used to call it "losing privileges."

Of course, my brothers were punished too. My mom once added weeks and weeks of grounding to one of them because he adamantly refused to comply. He stood defiantly as the situation escalated and rage filled the kitchen until he walked away with months of TV privileges lost, not allowed to go out and see his friends for what felt to my child's brain like an eternity.

I also remember being punished by people who weren't my parents. By teachers, coaches, and other family members. I remember being viciously shamed while my mom, who had the flu, threw up in the bathroom. This adult family member told me that it was my fault my mom was throwing up, and I remember feeling sick to my stomach for her, the shame of it all feeling like it would rip me apart. That must have been twenty-five years ago, and yet I still remember it vividly.

Maybe you remember being punished too; being hit, ignored, or shamed. Maybe your parents took away your stuff or
locked you in a room. Maybe they grounded you for months
like my brother. Maybe it was much, much worse.

After working with thousands of parents, I've heard many
stories of punishments far more severe than what I've experienced. Punishments involving extreme humiliation, physical
deprivation, violence, and other things that constitute abuse
or neglect.

For as long as any of us can remember, punishment has
been a staple of parenting. Most people cannot begin to imagine a way of raising children effectively without correcting
their problematic behavior with punishment. I know I couldn't.
When we messed up as kids, almost all of us were met with
time-outs, yelling, love withdrawal, shame, or, in the worst
cases, physical violence.

This shouldn't surprise us. The prevailing cultural myth of
Western European society for almost the last 2,500 years is
that if we, as a society, don't control people, they'll run amuck
and wind up jobless, homeless, incarcerated, and generally
speaking *ruining it* for the rest of us. And the myth continues
that the way to make sure people don't turn out like that is
punishment. It's baked into our religious frameworks, educational institutions, and "justice" system.

I used to believe that myth and likely would have kept on
punishing my kids had I not encountered an amazing parent
educator on the path to becoming a licensed foster parent.
One day, while watching the training videos with my wife, the
educator leading the training, a foster parent herself for the
last two decades, said something that shocked me.

"Punishment doesn't work on these kids. You have to *connect*
with them to help them to adjust their problematic behaviors."

I was taken aback. The population of kids we were preparing to foster had *more* behavioral issues than any kids I had ever known. They regularly hit and bit. They lashed out, stole, and destroyed property. They cussed and screamed and said hurtful things. Many had been suspended or expelled from school. Surely, if *anyone* needed a little punishment it was them. . . . Right?

Wrong, according to this expert.

These kids were traumatized. The parenting techniques you had to employ to work with them effectively had to be *exceptionally good*. Punishment, this trainer seemed to be saying, was an ineffective parenting tactic that didn't work *at all*. Punishment wasn't teaching kids to behave well; their parental relationships were. If anything, punishment was getting in the way.

This experience made me question everything I thought I knew about punishment and inspired me to dig deeper to find a better way—one that aligned with my desire to be an emotionally healthy, effective parent. And so, like any modern-day explorer on a quest for knowledge, I turned to the source of all truth and knowledge: Google. With a quick search, I was overwhelmed by a deluge of articles, books, podcasts, and online courses, all promising to hold the key to conscious, peaceful, gentle, respectful, responsive (or whatever else you want to call it) parenting. I drank in the sea of information, hoping to find the answers I so desperately sought.

But I couldn't help but feel a growing sense of *disappointment*. Much of what I encountered was vague, too abstract, or simply impractical for the real chaos of everyday parenting, and almost all of them avoided the elephant in the room: punishment. Normal parents like me needed tools and strategies to make a tangible difference in our daily interactions with our children, and if punishment was a bad way to discipline, then I wanted to know the better way.

It frustrated me to read about the importance of emotional connection and empathy without a roadmap for how to achieve these lofty ideals in the midst of tantrums, spilled juice, and sleepless nights. In moments of frustration and shame, I struggled to make any progress in myself or my relationship with my child, and I constantly found myself reverting to my old, reactive, *punitive* ways.

It took me years but one day, I found the missing puzzle piece. If I was going to truly embrace this new way of parenting, I had to ditch punishment for good. And to do that, I was going to have to understand my child and myself much better. Without examining and often confronting the core beliefs stored deep in my subconscious brain that underpinned my parenting approach, I was attempting to address a deeply rooted issue with a superficial fix. Without understanding where my child's behavior was coming from and why it was so triggering to me, parenting scripts and toddler tricks were just a Band-Aid on a bullet hole. I had to uncover how the mindsets around behavior and punishment from my own upbringing had become the "default settings" for my parenting.

This book is born out of the realization that there are countless parents out there, just like me, who crave practical guidance and brain-based, real-world solutions. It's a testament to the belief that all of us can heal, grow, and become more than we could ever imagine.

In this book, I'll take you through this very journey, step by step. Together, we'll dive into the core of punishment-free parenting, dispelling the myths that may be holding you back, and equipping you with actionable brain-centric strategies to create lasting change for your family.

Why Am *I* Writing This Book?

I'm not a scientist or an expert with a string of letters after my name. I'm just a parent who has enough academic training on how to research and how to separate good evidence-based advice from trendy nonsense.

While I haven't spent years conducting experiments in a lab or critiquing academic papers, I've been in the trenches, facing the everyday challenges of parenthood head-on. I've grappled with the same doubts, fears, and frustrations that many parents face. I've been through the ups and downs of trying to implement these strategies in my actual life. In short, I've walked the walk, and I continue to do so every day.

What truly sets me apart is my unique perspective as a pastor. I understand if that scares you, but hear me out before you throw this book across the room. This book has *no religious content,* but I'm convinced my perspective as a pastor has made a huge difference in my work with parents.

I've spent the years since my formal seminary training counseling and guiding people through the process of deconstructing unhelpful and even harmful narratives, often from their childhoods. I've learned how to create space for new, more fruitful beliefs and paradigms and help others do the same. My work as a parenting educator consistently draws parallels to those parts of my job: I walk with people as they face the deep and often disconcerting reality that what they learned in childhood might not be as helpful, fruitful, or, indeed, true, as they once assumed.

In this book, as in my work with parents at Whole Parent, we'll dig into the neuroscience and go into the deep, sometimes dark, aspects of our inner worlds. It's a place I'm comfortable going with people and it's the place we must go if we want real, lasting change. I'm here to walk with you through the journey of revisiting those challenging places with understanding and compassion.

But Will It Work for Me?

You might be asking yourself if it's really worth all this work. Is punishment-free parenting actually going to make a difference? Because, let's be honest, how do I even know if this process will work for you like it worked for me and my kids?

Well, that brings me to the next part of my story.

Once I started to immerse myself in the process of unraveling the myth of punishment deeply rooted in my own upbringing and cultural history, I began to notice a remarkable shift in the way I interacted with my children. My parenting journey became a whole lot easier, more enjoyable, and more *effective* once I ditched punishment and stopped running on autopilot.

This newfound understanding not only benefited my parenting but also transformed my experience of fatherhood. I was being punished by my punishments. Eager to share these breakthroughs, I talked to every new parent I could find. Shockingly, when they started to implement the steps I had taken to go punishment-free, the transformation in *their* parenting journey was often as profound as mine.

With their encouragement, I took the message to a broader audience on social media with few expectations. To my surprise, my story and process resonated with countless other parents who were navigating similar struggles. Thousands and thousands of comments and messages later I realized, *this really works for everyone.*

That overwhelming response from fellow parents eventually led me to establish a supportive membership community: the Whole Parent Membership. We came together each week, virtually, to discuss our real-life parenting challenges as they unfolded, and we did monthly workshops on topics ranging from How to Stop Yelling at Your Kids, to Sibling Rivalry and Toddler Tantrums, all without ever resorting to punishment.

From there, the number of parents seeking guidance and sharing their success stories grew exponentially, quickly turning from hundreds to thousands.

So here's the promise of this book—a curated and proven roadmap that has worked for countless parents like you and me to quit punishment for good. It's about more than just telling you to "connect empathetically with your child"; it's about retraining your *own* brain to see the world through a new lens, to understand the *why* behind the what of good discipline. If you come to this book looking for practical strategies that will help you curtail misbehavior in the moment and avoid unnecessary tantrums, this book will absolutely help you do that. If you are reading to learn how to survive toddlerhood or the teenage years without yelling yourself hoarse or resorting to ineffective punishments, this book will help you do that too. But if you're here looking to parent in a way that looks beyond the short-term compliance struggles of the immediate future and helps you raise kids for the long-term, not only when they're under your roof but for their whole lives, then I *wrote* this book for you. It's a journey I've embarked on, one that has changed me as a parent and a person, and I want nothing more than to share this transformation with you.

The Challenge and the Reward

That said, is this journey going to be hard? Yes, without a doubt. It requires you to show up and do the work, and that's not easy. You'll face moments of frustration, doubt, and setbacks along the way. Unlike other parenting "programs" or books that are primarily intended to gain short-term compliance, we're playing the long game. Punishment comes in all shapes and sizes, so it's going to be a lot more than learning what *not* to do. We have to learn how to think, act, and respond totally differently.

But here's the thing: The most rewarding journeys are almost always the ones that demand the most from us. When you commit to this path of punishment-free, whole parenting, you're making a promise to yourself and your children for a better, more connected future. The challenges and failures you'll face are not the obstacles in your way; they are the tools that mold you into a wiser, more compassionate parent.

Imagine a life where losing your cool becomes a rarity, and when you inevitably do lose it, you approach yourself with compassion, knowing it's an opportunity to actually *deepen* your connection with your child. Imagine a life where you can navigate your child's emotional storms with understanding and confident ease. Imagine a home filled with laughter, trust, and open communication rather than shame, blame, and broken relationships.

Now, picture your children growing up as self-assured, resilient individuals, possessing the emotional intelligence and inner strength to navigate life's inevitable challenges with confidence, empathy, and a profound understanding of their own worth. *That's* the *real* reward waiting on the other side of this journey.

What Exactly Is the WHOLE Parent Method?

So what exactly is the path to becoming a punishment-free parent? Here's what's to come in this book.

In the first chapter we'll ask, "What's so bad about punishment anyway?" It's a fair question. But the research is clear: Punishment doesn't work in the long term. And after this part, you're going to understand why.

Once we've deconstructed the false promise of punishment, we'll move on to my four pillars of punishment-free parenting. We'll dispel common misconceptions about punishment-free parenting and outline the truth about the four most central parenting pillars we all need to be successful. Those pillars are Curiosity, Modeling, Consequences, and Boundaries. Through these, I'll provide you with a clear understanding of what it means to be a punishment-free parent and how to embrace this approach without falling into the pitfalls of being overly permissive or becoming a dictator.

From there we will dig deeper into our own childhoods. This is where we will uncover the real reason going punishment-free is so challenging for most of us. This will also likely be the hardest part to read. Many people will undoubtedly put down the book here and miss out on the rest. But I encourage you to not be one of those people. The transformation on the other side is worth it, and I will be with you every step of the way.

Last is the most practical part of the entire book, the **5-Step WHOLE Parent Method for Punishment-Free Parenting**. I'll walk you through the step-by-step acronym (WHOLE) that empowers you to parent in those tough moments with empathy, connection, and emotional intelligence rather than punishment. Each step in the method is designed to be clear, easy to implement, and highly *effective*. You'll see immediate changes in your relationship with your children and your own emotional well-being.

Now if you're ready to transform the way you relate to your kids and become the parent you long to be, let's dive in.

Punishment-Free
PARENTING

1

The Problem with Punishment

Too often we forget that discipline really means to teach,
not to punish. A disciple is a student, not a recipient of
behavioral consequences.

—DANIEL J. SIEGEL, MD,

and TINA PAYNE BRYSON, PHD

If there seems to be one prevailing myth that defines old-school parenting, it is that punishment is the most effective way to control children's behavior and it is necessary for their development. It's most often my opposition to punishment that stops parents in their tracks. Most of us cannot imagine a world where parents discipline children effectively without punishing them. But I'm living proof that we live in that world.

Punishment, by definition, is a *retributive* action leveraged by an authority against someone who has done something that the authority believes is wrong. Punishments are used so that the offender is motivated not to offend in the future. Punishment looks back at a person's "bad behavior" and says, "I'm going to hurt you or (at least) make you uncomfortable to make sure you don't do that bad thing again."

The punishments parents use have taken many forms throughout human history. Here are a few of the most common:

- Corporal punishment (spanking, whupping, paddling, pinching, or otherwise physically hurting)
- Shame and disappointment ("You are a bad kid for doing that bad thing" or "I am disappointed in you")
- Yelling and/or scaring (*Why would you do that! I'm so mad at you right now!*)
- Love withdrawal ("I'm so mad at you right now, I don't want to be near you, go take a time-out!")
- Removal of positive reinforcement ("I'm taking away your tablet for a week!" or "You're grounded!")

I've listed these in order of most problematic to least, but make no mistake, they are *all* punishment. They all seek to harm or inconvenience a child in order to teach them a lesson.

If you want evidence as to how universal the authoritarian sentiment is that punishment is synonymous with teaching, consider how we tend to use the word "discipline." When I say discipline, people raised in authoritarian households, that is to say most people, immediately assume that I'm talking about punishment. "I was *disciplined* for taking my mom's lipstick and writing all over the bathroom mirror" means to most people, "I was *punished* for taking my mom's lipstick and writing all over the bathroom mirror." Ultimately, this is a misuse of the word "discipline." To discipline, coming from ancient Greek, means "to teach," not "to punish." Yet we have come to think of these words as synonymous because we have been convinced that punishment is not only *an* effective form of teaching, but the *most* effective form of teaching.

Psychologists and mental health experts have known for more than twenty years, for example, that corporal punishment—inflicting physical pain as a punishment—doesn't work. During the 1990s, research increasingly showed that inflicting pain on children as a means of discipline was both ineffective and had negative developmental outcomes.[1]

That said, most parents, especially in the United States, either were seemingly unaware of this research or didn't trust these findings. A composite of surveys conducted by the National Opinion Research Center shows that in the year 2000, U.S. parents who believed spanking was a *necessary* form of discipline outnumbered those who did not nearly three to one.[2] Six years later, the numbers had barely changed, with 72 percent of parents still convinced spanking was necessary.[3] Even more shocking is that another six years after that, the last time the survey was conducted, the number had shifted only slightly, with a whopping 70 percent of parents *still* believing that hitting children was a necessary part of parenting.[4] Let that sink in.

In 2012, when more than twenty countries had already made spanking illegal, 70 percent of American parents still believed it was not only permissible but *necessary* to spank children. Sweden, the first country to entirely ban corporal punishment, did so in 1979, over thirty years before that final survey was conducted. They did this because of the well-documented damaging effects violent punishments have on children.[5] Ironically, far from yielding positive long-term behavioral change, research consistently identifies that corporal punishment in childhood is linked to antisocial behavior, poor mental health, and even violence.[6]

If you take nothing else away from this book, let it be that, at the very least, corporal punishment is never an example of effective parenting and is, in fact, harmful to children.

What we rarely admit these days is that *all* punishments, including those that do not rely on physical pain, by definition, still rely on discomfort or psychological pain for the person being punished. While it seems the cultural tide is finally moving away from *corporal* punishment, we don't often consider that many other punishment techniques are also *painful.*[7]

When a parent shames, humiliates, or otherwise intentionally causes their child emotional distress (through isolation or insensitivity), the very same parts of their child's brain that would be activated by physical pain are activated by that emotional pain.[8] And what about grounding? That, too, creates *social* pain, which the brain also processes similarly.[9]

In fact, all punishment, at its core, is attempted discipline *by means of pain.*

The Impact of Punishment on Stress Response

To understand why punishment is not only an *un*productive way to discipline kids but is, in fact, *counter*productive, you first have to understand the body's stress response.

You have absolutely experienced this stress response phenomenon before, and you may even know it by its street names: "fight or flight" or "survival mode." What you might not know is that this response is triggered in our bodies by actual physiological processes.

One of the fundamental survival instincts all humans have arises from what is called the *autonomic nervous system.* The autonomic nervous system, specifically the sympathetic nervous system, is the part of your body that gets you ready to fight, flee, or freeze in dangerous situations. Buried deep in the core of your brain is a small, almond-shaped neural structure called the amygdala. The amygdala's job is to trigger automatic responses like feelings and memories.

When your body senses a threat, your amygdala triggers your autonomic nervous response to set off a cascade of hormones, chief among them epinephrine (adrenaline) and cortisol (the stress hormone), designed to get you ready to survive at all costs. Blood flow is withdrawn from the logic and reasoning centers of your brain and reallocated to your muscles. Your heart rate increases. You, in effect, stop thinking and prepare to *react*. Instead of making choices based on logic or careful reasoning, you start being run by the oldest parts of your brain—what many fondly call the "lizard brain."[10]

When this happens, the prefrontal cortex, the part of the brain with *higher order cognitive processes*—a fancy term for things like long-term decision making, moral reflection, abstract reasoning, critical thinking, and metacognition (thinking about what you're thinking about)—all have to take a backseat. The brain is prioritizing *survival* and *not* rational, moral, long-term decision making. When this process is activated, it happens so fast that your body actually sends you into survival mode faster than your cognition perceives it. Consider that for a moment. Put in the simplest terms, if your amygdala sees something that it thinks could hurt you, it hops into the driver's seat of your brain and takes control to save your life. (I know, it's got a real hero complex, that one.) The thing is, when the amygdala's driving, your brain isn't good at doing much else.

The reason our brains do this is to allow us to act *without* thinking. Thinking is actually pretty slow. It takes us about half a second to comprehend what our senses are telling us and then usually another half a second to make a decision about what to do. When confronted with a true threat to your life or well-being, you don't want to sit around considering your options like you're ordering DoorDash. You want to be able to act without thinking because a half-second lag can be the difference between life and death.

When I was seventeen and driving my 2002 Ford Focus with no antilock braking system down an icy Chicago side street coming up to a busy intersection, my lizard brain's ability to jump in and act instinctively probably saved my life. I pumped the brakes and corrected the car as it slid, narrowly avoiding two dumpsters and sliding to a halt just in time to avoid oncoming traffic. The whole thing happened so fast, my "thinking" brain didn't even really know what had happened. That's just one example from my life, and I bet you could identify several times when your lizard brain kept you alive too.

But the trade-offs can be rough.

Do you ever feel like you make irrational or even straight-up bad decisions when you're tired or scared or hungry or mad? That's your amygdala taking over when it probably doesn't need to. You make less-than-ideal decisions, focused on short-term gratification rather than long-term outcomes. When your brain is in survival mode, it's not concerned with the next twenty years; it's consumed with the next twenty seconds. The brain is no longer interested in learning anything that's not relevant for immediate survival.

Punishments, whether they rely on physical, mental, emotional, or relational pain, activate the stress response in our children. This is why punishments, in a way, *can't* provide long-term learning. Trying to *teach children a lesson* by sending them into their fight-or-flight response is totally ineffective.

That's why using punishment to discipline is not only *un-productive,* it's *counterproductive.*

The crazy thing is we can send our kids into survival mode over the mere *perception* of our frustration. The younger the brain, the less able it is to distinguish between real and perceived threats. This is because the part of their brain that sends them into fight or flight—their amygdala—is fully developed in toddlers, while the part of their brain that helps them to not go into survival mode over nothing won't be fully developed for two decades.

When things that aren't threats are perceived as dangerous, the body can respond inappropriately as a result. I call that "amygdala hijack." It's when the lizard brain, responsible for keeping your tiny human alive, jumps into the driver's seat and takes control of your child. When that happens, you can end up with a child ready to fight for their life (that is, to the death) because you brought them the wrong-shaped pasta.

But that's not the only reason punishment is ineffective. Punishment also teaches the wrong lesson in most cases. Let me give you an example.

The Real Lessons of Punishment

Your three-year-old child is at a park, playing in the sandbox with a dump truck alongside another child. The two start to compete over the truck, struggling to take turns (as basically all kids of that age do), and ultimately they start to fight over the truck. In the scuffle your child pushes the other child down, taking the truck. The other child starts to cry.

Pause for a moment and think about this situation as if it

had been you as a child. When and how would your parents
have intervened in the sandbox?

If you had old-school authoritarian parents, here are some
common ways:

1. If they were watching closely they might have swooped
   in to wrest the truck from you before even the onset of
   conflict, handing it to the other child and insisting that
   you "have to share."
2. If they were a little farther back or more distracted (perhaps reading a book), they might have intervened during the initial struggle to take the truck away from both
   kids. "You can't have this if you won't share."
3. Farther back still, they might have only intervened after
   you pushed the other child down, at which point they
   might have grabbed you by the arm, whipped you
   around, taken the truck away, and said firmly, "We do
   not hit! Do we have to leave the park? Now I'm giving
   him the truck, and if you do something like that again
   we're leaving."

Or, worse, perhaps they would have skipped all of that entirely and just given you a spanking.

Do any of these sound familiar? If you grew up in the '80s
or '90s, tactics like these probably sounded normal or even
right to you at some point in your life.

That's because what we experience as children becomes
our default understanding of the world, our factory default
settings, no matter how illogical (or in some cases immoral).
It's just the nature of having a developing brain.

But let's, for a moment, forget about the neuroscience and

the stress response. Let's just question what these "authoritarian" responses communicate to the three-year-old child.

1. I have the power to take your toys and give them to other people and I will use that power. Don't let me see you even considering doing something I don't like again. I am in charge; never forget that.
2. I don't trust you to navigate your own conflicts. If I see you beginning to have a conflict, I will intervene and assert my power. You cannot be trusted. You don't make decisions; you follow directions.
3. Me. Me. Me. Focus on Me. I have the power to hurt you or punish you. Don't look at the kid on the ground, look at me. I am the most important person in your world, and you made me mad. I have the power to hurt you, and if you're not careful, I will. How I feel about what you do is more important than the *actual impact* of what you do.

Do you see the secondary problem with disciplining by means of punishment? If discipline is about teaching, what does responding in these ways teach?

In this illustration there was an amazing opportunity to do some skill building, healthy relationship teaching, and empathy training—in other words, an opportunity to do some great *discipline*—but that opportunity is easily missed when we default to punishment in the service of control. Punishment-first parents, often in fight-or-flight mode themselves, rarely stop to consider what lesson they are even attempting to teach.

These parents allow their own frustrations (and often their

fear of judgment by other onlooking adults) to dictate their reaction. As a result, the child learns the wrong lesson:

"I am not responsible enough to make choices. My mom/dad controls me, and my goal should be to not upset them."

What most parents hope to teach in those situations is radically different:

"Sharing is important when you're playing with someone else. Pushing someone to get your way hurts them, and they may not want to play with you anymore."

But the punishment distracts kids from the lessons we are trying to teach them.

I am often asked, "Jon, even if it's not perfect, doesn't punishment ultimately still disincentivize bad behavior?"

In some cases it may but in order for a behavior to be disincentivized, the child has to connect the punishment with the behavior. Many times, if not *most* times, in young children that simply doesn't happen. Ask a child who was spanked for hitting their brother or coloring on the walls why they were spanked a week or two after the event. I have, and I can report that very often they're unable to give me a clear answer. Usually I'll get something vague like, "I was being bad/naughty," or, "I wasn't listening," or even "I made my mommy/daddy mad." Why? Because the moment the parent resorted to violence, the child went into fight-or-flight mode. Their brain stopped trying to learn and started focusing on survival.

And this is why most traditional authoritarian punishments don't work long-term: They rely on *hurting* the offender to make a point. That pain can be physical, as with hitting or spanking, or it could be emotional, as with shaming or humiliation. It can even be social or relational—as with love withdrawal or purposefully ignoring your child, which takes advantage of the fact that children's survival instincts include knowing that they are ultimately reliant on their parents.

Remember that the exact same parts of the brain that process physical pain are also the ones that process emotional pain.[11] That means their brain will often interpret shame, humiliation, or rejection *as pain*, and the "thinking" part of their brain will effectively get shut off. When that happens, kids enter a decidedly "nonreceptive" state. We will learn how to help kids who are in these states later in the book, but for now, I just want you to grasp this: When you punish a kid to teach a lesson, you shut off the part of their brain that learns.

The Irony of Punishment

These aren't the only issues with punishment. When parents use punishment as the primary (or even *only*) deterrent for a problematic behavior, ironically, kids are conditioned to stop caring about the impact of their behaviors and hyperfocus on whether they'll get caught and punished.

In 2013 Daniel Nagin, a criminologist at Carnegie Mellon University, wrote a summary of what we know about deterring crime as of the twenty-first century. He found that, when considering punishment as a deterrent, crime is primarily deterred not by the *severity* or *nature* of the punishment but by the *likelihood of being caught*.[12]

If you primarily attempt to deter your kid's problem behaviors with punishment, they may behave when they know you're watching. But when you're not? All bets are off. In fact, I bet you have at least a handful of examples of kids you knew in high school whose strict parents had no *clue* what their kids got up to when they weren't watching.

I can't tell you the number of kids I went to high school with who were raised in authoritarian, punishment-heavy environments whose parents were convinced that the kids were perfect, compliant little angels. They got straight A's, had high standardized test scores, started on the varsity team, and made sure to do all the extracurricular activities that looked great on a transcript. And then on the weekend, while their parents were otherwise distracted, they slipped out of their basement window and went completely nuts, engaging in all sorts of high-risk activities. One Monday morning, I arrived at school to find out that one of my classmates had gotten drunk or high or maybe both and proceeded to drive her dad's BMW straight through the local Dunkin' Donuts. Yes, *through*.

If you parent in such a way that *you* become the primary incentive for your child to behave or make good choices, I have some tough love for you: You won't always be there. And when you're not there, your child will lack the skills, resources, and reasoning to make healthy and fruitful choices.

If your kid was afraid of getting in trouble when they were six years old, when your kid is in *real* trouble at sixteen, do you think they're going to call you? Of course not. Parents are often the last people on earth teenagers will tell when they've made a mistake precisely because we have conditioned them to think that way.

Don't get me wrong, teenage brains are *far* more advanced than toddler brains, but they still have some growing to do. One place teenage brains still need to grow is in the ability to accurately weigh the long-term consequences of their actions. Teens just haven't developed enough yet to weigh causes and effects accurately. This is why people often say that teens "think they're invincible." They don't. They just have an underdeveloped prefrontal cortex. For a sixteen-year-old, risking their life by driving home drunk from a party or getting in the car with a drunk friend behind the wheel to avoid their parents' finding out they were there may seem reasonable—*especially* if they're worried about how rough on them their parents will be if they call for a ride.

I can't stress this enough. When we condition young children to hide their mistakes from us for fear of punishment, we set them up to hide much larger and more dangerous things from us later in life. On the other hand, the toddler who receives help cleaning up the kitchen disaster they made without permission instead of a spanking grows up into the teenager who calls for help when they go to a party without permission and their designated driver gets drunk.

Parents who punish are choosing (knowingly or unknowingly) to stop, prevent, or curtail negative behaviors in the short term rather than putting their energy into the long-term relational, moral, and emotional development of their children.

Parenting with Spectators

Why do we make this short-term choice? One big reason is that we don't want to be perceived as a bad parent (or have our child perceived as a bad kid). The social pressure to get your kid in line, often through our factory default methods, can be all we care about in the tense moments.

It's like being really hungry. When you're driving home from that late dance recital you barely made it to because work was a nightmare (which is also, by the way, why you missed lunch and wound up scarfing down a bag of chips and a candy bar at 3:00 P.M.) and you're passing all of these fast food restaurants . . . it's hard not to stop.

You know that pulling into that drive-thru means you'll have a 1,300-calorie burger and fries in your hand in T-minus 3.5 minutes. In those moments, your blood sugar is low, triggering your amygdala to take over, and it's all you can think about. In fact, maybe you'll get two burgers. . . .

Never mind that you have the ingredients at home for a delicious and nutritious meal that won't make you feel like garbage two hours later. Never mind that you were supposed to be cutting out high-cholesterol foods and red meat. Never mind that your kids in the backseat will scream nonstop for ice cream, which they usually get at this burger joint, and the ride home is objectively going to be way harder whether you got them the ice cream or said no.

But you want that burger now. It's all-consuming. Screw the long term; you need that food right now.

It's why I am an objectively worse parent at the grocery store than I am at home. When parenting feels like a spectator sport, we often get triggered, even though that, too, is just another example of your amygdala's overreactions.

So we punish. Not because it's effective or productive, but because we're not in control.

And that's the great irony of all of this. The vicious cycle of it all. We get triggered and then we punish; they get triggered by our punishment and learn nothing. They do it again and we get triggered again—this time doubly so because they're also "not listening." And so we punish all the harder.

But I Turned Out Fine. . . .

When I talk about going punishment-free with parents who grew up being severely punished, the single biggest objection is, "But my parents punished me and look at me, I turned out OK. It couldn't have been *that* bad." In my experience, this sentiment seems especially if not almost exclusively poignant in adults who were not just victims of punishment generally but specifically of violent punishment.

I've also heard it expressed as justification by parents of adult children who attempt to excuse especially harsh parenting tactics they used when those children were young. The number of times someone has commented "Well, I hit my kids and they all became doctors" on one of my posts outlining the long-term consequences of physical violence on children, one might think that being hit was a prerequisite of medical school.

All this to say, if you or your partner has used the "but I turned out fine . . ." justification, I get it. One of the things that makes us human is our ability to make meaning out of a host of problematic situations to overcome their potentially devastating effects. This ability to integrate our experiences into a comprehensive and consistent narrative is one of the most powerful tools we possess to process trauma and overcome its consequences. You may have had a caregiver who loved you. They may have connected with you deeply, provided for you, and might even still have a positive relationship with you to this day. And that same person may have also hurt you intentionally. Now you have to reconcile the cognitive dissonance that comes with having the person who loves you and is responsible for your safety hurt you "for your own good." In many cases, that violence also may have had religious undertones. It's no wonder that our brains, in an effort to protect us, turn those traumatic experiences into something *meaningful*.

If that is your story, I want to tell you that you did not need to be hit to learn any lesson that you learned.

The ability to make meaning out of your trauma is less of a testament to punishment as a means of discipline than it is to the resilience of the human spirit. You did not turn out "fine" because of your parents' inability to regulate their emotions or teach you in ways that unnecessarily involved pain. None of us are better for the violence that we received at the hands of our parents.

People who were hit in childhood (or shamed, excessively yelled at, humiliated, and similar) often become successful in spite of going through those experiences, not because of them. No one becomes a good, passionate, and compassionate doctor *because* their parents hit them as toddlers, but I imagine many people who might have become doctors didn't precisely *because* they were hit. The idea that we "turned out OK" in spite of our parents' problematic punishments is not a reason to justify or repeat them. We can and should do better.

Setting the Record Straight

Before we move on to how we can raise resilient kids without resorting to ineffective and potentially damaging punishments, I want to address one of the most common misconceptions about punishment-free parenting. This misconception is that parents who don't use punishments don't hold their children accountable. While that is certainly true for some permissive parents out there, it is definitely not what I'm offering you as the alternative to punishment. Before we get there, I want to say that I totally get where criticisms like this come from. Most of us cannot imagine accountability without punishment. Moreover, there is a tendency, when you deconstruct from any worldview or paradigm—parenting or otherwise—to "over-correct." If you overcorrect from a compliance-, punishment-, or achievement-based parenting philosophy, the logic follows that you might accidentally foster a spirit of noncompliance, zero consequences, and low achievement in your child. The thinking continues that a child raised in that way would have zero respect for authority, no motivation, and likely wind up doing something to land themselves in jail. After all, that was the justification offered by many pro-punishment advocates.

Before I go on, can I just point out how pessimistic a worldview like this is about human nature? By this logic, the only reason all of us don't steal and cheat and murder all the time is because we were raised to *fear* authority and punishment.

I don't believe that, and I hope you don't either.

A worldview like this also assumes that the best way to teach respect and cooperation is through disrespect and force. What we know from the research—and what I can personally attest to in my own parenting—is that the best way to teach respect is actually by modeling respect, something we'll talk about in chapter 3.

The issue is that many parents falsely equate *respect* with fear and unwavering, unquestioning compliance.

This worldview also seems to imply that most if not all the people who end up doing the truly harmful things—assault, murder, and so on—were raised in a home that practiced punishment-free parenting. Nothing can be further from the truth. In fact, extensive research shows that kids raised in homes where they were not fundamentally safe, where they were subjected to neglect or abuse, especially physical violence, are precisely the ones who tend to commit the most heinous crimes.[13] This is part of the growing body of research we've already talked about that suggests that the more a child is violently punished or subjected to extreme emotional pain as punishment, the more likely they are to engage in anti-social and violent behavior as teens and adults. This theory, usually called the "cycles of violence theory," has been around since the late 1980s and gains more evidence testifying to its validity every year.

So that's the problem, or better said, "problems," with punishment. Over the next four chapters you'll learn how to build a new, better foundation. One that will allow you to discipline effectively, including how to hold your children accountable, without punishment, and while still avoiding the trap of permissiveness. Buckle up. It's going to be a journey.

2

Get Curious, Not Furious

Be curious, not judgmental.
—UNKNOWN

A quote, often misattributed to Walt Whitman, goes like this: "Be curious, not judgmental."

My favorite scene in one of my favorite shows revolves around this advice. Ted, the titular main character of the Emmy-winning show *Ted Lasso,* gives an impassioned speech all about this quote while playing darts against the primary antagonist in the first season. Ted reflects that none of the judgmental boys of his youth who bullied him and picked on him were ever curious. They asked no questions, and because they asked no questions, they knew next to nothing about him. The revelation came when Ted realized that when someone bullies you without knowing anything about you, it means it has nothing to do with you, and *everything to do with them.*

The moment I saw this scene, I fell in love with the quote. It speaks to a fundamental truth of life and especially parenting.

The antidote to judgment, and often the punishment that follows, is curiosity.

The Antidote to Judgment

At the core of being punishment-free is the principle that we have to stop approaching our kids with judgment and must instead get curious. With our kids, judgment can come in many shapes and sizes, none of which help us to parent any better or help our children to self-regulate or to learn. The most common way I see parents "judging" the behaviors of their children is by allowing themselves to be triggered by those behaviors and acting *aggressively,* usually with threats or punishments. This is why, from here on out, instead of saying, "Be curious, not judgmental," I'm going to say: *Get curious, not furious*.

Instead of getting furious when our kids misbehave, get dysregulated, or generally just get on our very last nerve, we must choose to become caregivers who seek first to understand.

I want to come right out and say, this is not an easy change for any of us to make. We were children once too, and as children we developed deeply ingrained neural pathways that guide our factory-default parenting. If your parents did not meet your behavior with a posture of curiosity during your most formative years, it is going to take conscious and deliberate intentionality on your part to break that cycle. It's going to mean employing all of the tactics and tricks available to you— those taught in this book, and hard-won skills you have acquired elsewhere—not to act on your unconscious impulse to meet your children's problematic behaviors with anger, judgment, and punishment, and instead engage them thoughtfully and curiously. You may have to take one (or five) centering breaths. You may have to employ a therapy device like grounding. You might just need to walk away and gather yourself before you choose to respond, rather than react. Whatever you have to do, I promise you it is worth it. Because good discipline starts by getting to the *root* of your children's behaviors.

Understanding Behavior

The first thing I want you to understand about your kid's behavior is that all behavior is just communication. A lot of that communication in kids is happening without their awareness. Contrary to popular belief, kids rarely "choose" to misbehave in order to be manipulative or malicious. More often parents are just experiencing the outpouring of something else going on underneath the surface. That's why I often tell parents (and have to remind myself fifty times a day) *your kid's not giving you a hard time; they're having a hard time.*

So what are these behaviors communicating?

Certain behaviors communicate that we have conditioned our children in some less than ideal way. I may yell when I get upset because my dad yelled when he got upset. He yelled because his dad did too. My kids are far more likely to yell when they get upset because I do.

Other behaviors communicate the developmental stage our children are in during a given time. Here are two examples.

Kids between the ages of eighteen months and three years

tend to hit and bite. They do this because their physical development outpaces their verbal development. This seems especially true, from my experience working with parents, of younger siblings who, without adequate speech development, have to vie for the attention of their parents and often compete with bigger, stronger, smarter older siblings for toys and snacks. These toddlers learn that one way to communicate or gain control over a larger opponent is through violence—an undoubtedly problematic behavior that, on its own, usually quickly goes away as they outgrow it and their verbal development catches up.

Another common one that happens with kids a little older is lying. Many kids over the age of eight (and in fact teens and adults) lie to avoid punishment or social alienation. This is communicating a need for survival. Others lie because they've seen lying modeled.

But then there are younger kids, usually four or five years old, who grow up in punishment-free, positive-discipline households with parents who do not model dishonesty and yet still go through a "lying phase." This is because they're suddenly developmentally able to make up elaborate stories but lack the developmental reasoning to understand that saying something does not necessarily make it true.

In other words, lying for kids of this age is often completely devoid of malice. Given their blossoming imagination, they sometimes blur the lines between reality and make-believe. That's all that's happening. They might make up stories or provide imaginative explanations for otherwise mundane events. When they claim these tales as truth, it's not always a deliberate attempt to deceive but rather an exploration of their expanding cognitive and imaginative abilities and an exercise in understanding objective "truth" (something they will become obsessed with in later childhood). Their lying is not an example of intentional deception, or moral failing. It is just a snapshot of their developmental stage.

In both the lying and the hitting/biting examples, most of us have been conditioned to lead with judgment, attempting to correct the behavior without getting to the underlying cause. We see the symptom and attempt to deal with it alone without ever getting curious about where it's coming from.

By far, the most common source of misbehavior is the communication of *unmet* needs.

Seeing the Unmet Needs

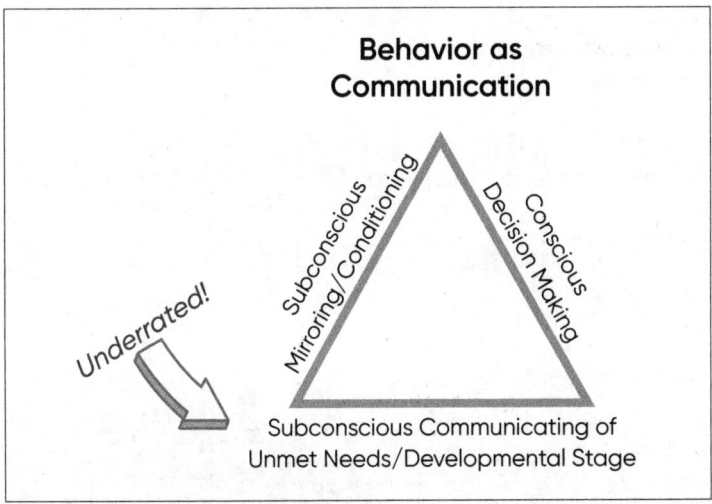

Behavior as Communication

Subconscious Mirroring/Conditioning

Conscious Decision Making

Underrated!

Subconscious Communicating of
Unmet Needs/Developmental Stage

Every human being has certain biological and psychological needs. Some of these are obvious: food, shelter, water, oxygen. Others are more subtle and nuanced: safety, belonging, love, respect, a sense of purpose.

Probably the most well-known list of these needs comes from a paper published in 1943 by Abraham Maslow called

"A Theory of Human Motivation."[1] It was and continues to be one of the most audacious and awesome papers I've ever read. Maslow attempts to explain basically all of human behavior and psychopathology as our innate desire to have our fundamental human needs met.

Most people will never read the actual paper, but at some point they will come across a graphic or explanation of the hierarchy the paper proposes.

The hierarchy is usually represented by a color-coded pyramid graphic, but I think it's actually easier to understand as a ladder or using the following stair step graphic.

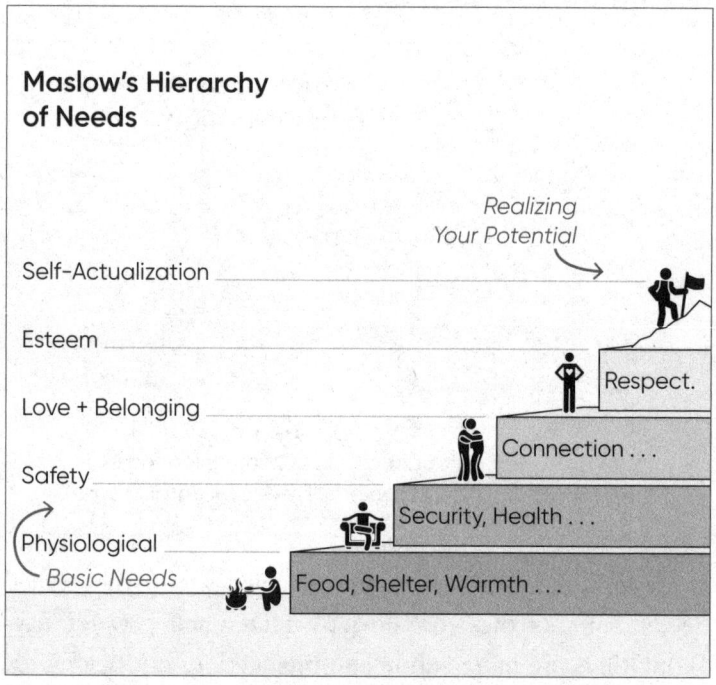

Maslow's Hierarchy of Needs

Self-Actualization — *Realizing Your Potential*

Esteem — Respect.

Love + Belonging — Connection . . .

Safety — Security, Health . . .

Physiological / *Basic Needs* — Food, Shelter, Warmth . . .

Maslow theorized that humans have an ascending pattern of needs, beginning with physiological needs like food, water, shelter, and warmth, and moving up through other secondary evolutionary psychological needs (safety), psychosocial needs (love and belonging), and eventually higher-order needs such as self-esteem (being autonomous and respected) and individual consciousness and fulfillment (purpose).

If a human doesn't get their lower needs met, they cannot move on to the higher needs. That's why I like the progressive needs graphics more than the pyramids (which frankly remind me of the food pyramid of my 1990s childhood).

For example, if a person is starving, they won't care about skipping a colonoscopy. Sure, both colon cancer and starvation can kill you, but one will kill you much faster. We default to meeting the lower needs.

A lot of this should resonate with what we've already talked about related to the brain's stress response—and specifically the brain's natural prioritization of survival (the most primitive need we have) over learning or moral reasoning. But it goes beyond that.

This prioritization of more basic needs, along with developmental needs, makes up the third leg of the behavior triangle you saw above. Humans—children and adults—behave in given ways to *get their needs met*. Some of these manifest as evolutionary survival drives, but most are more subtle things. Here are some examples:

- The teenage boy with body image issues who doesn't feel attractive posts "thirst traps" on social media for likes and affirmation he's not manifesting internally.
- The kindergarten girl bites her classmate to get the attention of the adult in the room when she isn't getting enough attention from the adults at home.

- The romantic partner who no longer feels seen and valued sleeps with their coworker so they can feel wanted and valued again.

The higher levels are where the hierarchy gets far more complicated and nuanced. When we don't have to worry as much about the first two categories of physiological and safety needs, our behavior becomes harder to understand.

Most adults in the developed world today tend to exist in the upper three levels, occasionally dipping back down into safety but by and large staying above those more basic needs. While it makes perfect sense that we probably aren't going to go looking for someone to date if we're dying of thirst, we don't often consider that *belonging* comes before *esteem* on the hierarchy. What this means is that, as inherently social creatures, we would rather be *disrespected* as part of the group than be *respected* and alone. It's this characteristic of human psychology that allows for toxic bosses and partners to continue their patterns of abuse. It often goes against our hierarchy to leave our tribe, even when the tribe is hurting us or insisting that punishment is the only way to discipline.

For our kids, when their most basic needs are not being met, they often communicate that to their caregivers through what we might identify as misbehavior. Here are some examples:

- A toddler cries when you leave the room because they lack the developmental capacity, called *object permanence,* to know that you didn't cease to exist when you're no longer in their presence, so their fear of abandonment throws them into emotional chaos.
- A first grader who is hungry lacks the brain development

and predictive ability to push down that feeling when the teacher says lunch is "only twenty minutes from now" and they act out.

- A four-year-old who feels starved for connection and attention lacks the developmental capacity for patience to let Mom finish that email before she plays and so throws a tantrum.

- An eight-year-old who lacks the prefrontal cortex development to rationalize his way out of humans' inbuilt separation anxiety is afraid of being alone in the dark. For 99.9 percent of human history, and in much of the world even today, prepubescent children were *never* away from caregiving adults at night. His evolutionary survival instincts are sounding a five-alarm fire because his parents are not in the same room as he is, and so he has a meltdown.

We adults can have many of our unmet needs *somewhat* satisfied by our brain's ability to say, "Hey, this isn't forever. The next meal is in a couple hours . . ." or, "I know I *feel* scared of the pitch-black basement at night, but really, logically, there's nothing to be scared of." (Cue forcing yourself to walk slowly the first couple of steps—because, after all, you are a rational adult—before breaking into a full-on sprint toward the stairs and the safety of the well-lit part of the house.)

For our kids, it is different.

Their orbital medial prefrontal cortex (OMPFC for short), the part of the adult brain that can override what we *feel* with what we *think,* isn't yet developed enough to win that battle in their mind.[2] So when they have an unmet need, it often comes out in less-than-ideal, destructive ways.

Why do the unmet fundamental physiological, safety, and

even connection-based needs tend to come out in these ways? Two main reasons.

First, behaving problematically is usually more likely to alert the adult caregiver to a need faster than most other means. This is why parents who are particularly responsive and attuned to the communication and needs of their children generally have kids who don't whine, tantrum, or misbehave as much. (But all kids still do that stuff sometimes.) So in this way, being responsive with curiosity, while sometimes taking more time in the short term, usually leads to having to deal with fewer difficult and frankly annoying behaviors in the long run.

Second, they're responding to needs lower on the hierarchy. When they're hungry and their little bodies are literally afraid they might not get enough calories to survive, they don't care if they're perceived as rude or ungrateful. They are in survival mode, and they are going to act to get their needs met.

I want to take a quick detour specifically into attention and separation needs. I can't prove it yet, but I believe that many of the "love and belonging" needs in prepubescent children are actually better understood as *safety needs*.

Kids, throughout all of human history—literally hundreds of thousands of years of evolution—have fundamentally *not* been safe when they are not connected to loving, attentive, adult caretakers. This role has not always been fulfilled exclusively by children's parents, but it has always been filled by adults. Kids just intrinsically know that they're not safe when they're alone.

The reason for this is that primates (and especially *Homo sapiens*) take significantly longer to reach maturity than other species. Juveniles cannot fend for themselves, repel threats, and reproduce on their own. According to Dr. Suzana Herculano-Houzel, a neuroscientist at Vanderbilt, the reason for this is because of, you guessed it, our amazing brains.[3]

The human brain, according to her research, has by far the most cortical neurons of any species. In fact, our brain is so incredibly complex and active that roughly 25 percent of the energy we use every day—a higher percentage than any other species—is used by our brains. In order to make enough room for that energy to be expended, our bodies have to grow and develop more slowly.

Combine this with the fact that humans have to be born earlier (relatively speaking) in gestation so that our disproportionately large heads with our disproportionately large and complex brains can fit through our mothers' very proportionally sized birth canals, and you get totally dependent little newborns who don't get their first tastes of autonomy in the first days of life, as many species do. Their brains won't fully develop for a quarter of a century.[4]

What this all means for us, as parents, is that our kids are necessarily dependent on us: They know it in their DNA. You already knew that too, but I want you to really stop and think about it.

Without you, your newborn might live only days. Your toddler, maybe weeks. Your prepubescent child, if truly alone, months at best. You might not like to think about that, but they know this instinctively and so their need for your attention, connection, and love feel to them like a life-and-death matter just like shelter, warmth, or food.

When parents really begin to understand and embody that all behavior is communication and therefore much of their children's misbehavior is simply communicating unmet needs, it can literally change their lives.

Why Punishment *Seems* to Work

Up to this point I haven't really talked about the elephant in the room. I've outlined why punishment doesn't work for effectively disciplining kids, but I haven't identified why it *seems* to work.

I said in chapter 1 that all punishment relies, in the end, on some form of pain. It's our hierarchy of needs that makes pain seem effective. Pain, whether it's social pain, emotional pain, physical pain, or even the *fear* of disconnection and rejection from your primary caregiver (relational pain), overrules the higher cognitive needs on the hierarchy. This is why raising your voice or threatening will frequently grab the attention of your child in the moment, even if, in the long term, the punishment is far less effective than the other alternative discipline methods I'm proposing.

You may get their attention and even their compliance in the short term, but in the long term you're not setting them up for success. The best way to do that is to consider what it is that your child is attempting to communicate to you through their problematic behaviors and then seek to address those. So with that in mind, let's look at some of the most common unmet needs that kids and adolescents face that often manifest as misbehavior.

The Most Common Culprits of Misbehavior

The first four needs to start with, which appear in almost every good parenting book I've ever read, make up the acronym HALT: Hungry, Angry, Lonely, and Tired. When kids are hungry, angry, lonely, or tired, their propensity to "misbehave" or "throw a tantrum" increases exponentially.

I had a recurring situation with my three-year-old. He was having frequent tantrums and meltdowns over seemingly innocuous things. I tried to chalk it all up to amygdala hijack— I mean, he's three, it felt like the obvious answer—but it seemed to be happening at the same time every day, around 9:30 in the morning. Too frequently to be coincidental.

It took my brilliant wife to realize what was really happening. The way our schedules work, I'm in charge of waking up with the kids and getting them breakfast. Over time, I had moved breakfast later and later until sometimes it wasn't until after 8:00. My three-year-old was often the first up, usually a little after 6:00. This meant he was already so hungry by 8:00 that he (and kids do this for some reason) no longer even wanted to eat.

It seemed fine to me. We operate in our house from evidence-based nutritional practices that can be summarized as, "You offer them food and they eat it if they're hungry and you don't push it if they're not because their body knows better than you." If my son wasn't eating breakfast, that was his body telling me he didn't need to eat. At least that was what I thought. . . .

But he was actually really hungry, and every day at 9:30 he was getting "hangry" and misplacing the discomfort of being hungry on whatever we were trying to do. If we were getting changed for an outing, he was obstinately opposed to the clothes we picked out. When we tried to give him the autonomy to pick out his own clothes (a typically excellent toddler hack) he would devolve into screams and crying. If we stayed in and tried to do art or play a game or even have a dance party, he would inevitably throw a tantrum about some random tiny thing. Even if he had total and complete control and everything was going his way, by 9:30, we were in chaos.

One morning I'd had it. Punishment-brain kicked in and I finally screamed, *"I don't care if you want it! We don't have it!"*

He desperately wanted to wear black pants as I recall. . . .

That was the morning my wife finally figured it out. I was so caught up in trying to fix the symptoms that I never got to the root problem and eventually got *furious*. It took someone else being *curious* to solve the case.

The next morning the waffle iron was hot by 6:30. Before his brother was even up he had an entire waffle, some pieces of vegan sausage, and a cup of orange juice. In the months since, I've had essentially no morning meltdowns as long as he's fed before 7:00. My toddler was not trying to be difficult; he was communicating an unmet need in the only way he knew how.

Similarly, when our kids miss their nap, they're going to be easily triggered and probably act erratically. When they come home angry about something that happened at school, they might take it out on us. When they feel alone and isolated, they will almost always turn to some form of attention-seeking behavior around the safest adults in their life. And as I've learned, when Dad forgets to feed them and they've gone sixteen hours since they last ate, they're going to rage about the color of their pants.

Our job as parents is to become curious, not furious. We must become *unmet needs detectives*. The behaviors that rear up and bite us are not signs of our children's tainted immortal souls (this is actually what is taught in a handful of religious parenting spaces even to this day). They are signs of our children's developing brains and often their deep unmet needs.

When we fail to remember that our children are not *giving us* a hard time, they're *having* a hard time, we react with punishment and fail to meet the underlying need.

Here is a list of common unmet needs, beyond HALT, that are likely the culprit behind many of your children's problematic behaviors:

- **Stagnation.** Kids have never been more inactive than they are today. Many kids spend a majority of their free time engrossed in tablets and phones. They have very little time for the imaginative and active play their bodies so desperately crave. Team sports have broadly replaced "free play" and pickup games where children expended far more of their energy in years past. *Kids made to sit are kids who throw fits.*

- **Hurt/Sick.** Kids who are hurting, emotionally or physically, are going to have a harder time regulating feelings. A scrape on the knee is easily forgotten by most kids, but for some highly sensitive kids, it may feel overwhelming and impact their mood and behaviors for the rest of the day. Additionally, sick kids often act out as a first sign of illness.

- **Autonomy/Control.** Toddlers and teens especially have an inbuilt need for autonomy and control. As they first separate from their parents in toddlerhood as their bodies and brains develop, they often engage in autonomy-seeking behaviors which look like "misbehaving" or "disrespect" but are actually a natural and essential part of development. Similarly, teens have an inbuilt desire to be distinct and in fact *distant* from their parents, which is an evolutionary instinct to increase genetic diversity in our species and limit inbreeding. Parents who try to clamp down to limit this autonomy seeking and self-expression are met with both "rebellious" behaviors and potential mental health complications.

- **Safety.** Beyond being lonely or hungry, there is also an innate need for safety in kids. Humans, especially new humans, are skittish. We don't like the dark, or strangers, or big animals, or weird-tasting foods. But safety goes far beyond just that. According to a 2000 study on 285 kids, average age around ten, raised in South Central L.A., kids who grew up exposed to or as victims of violence showed increased likelihood of antisocial behavior and decreased emotional regulation.[5] Without the assurance of safety, kids will naturally act out more.

- **Disconnection from Nature.** Believe it or not, there is a growing body of research that indicates that kids' being out in nature helps them to stay more regulated and less likely to misbehave. Similar to "stagnation" above, this is a sign of our times, and it will take intentional effort on the part of parents to get kids back out in nature. I can personally attest that "Nature Deficit Disorder," as coined by Richard Louv in *Last Child in the Woods*, is a real thing with very real effects, especially on kids.

I want to end this chapter, which began with a reference to one of my favorite relatively recent TV shows, with an analogy using one of my favorite less recent shows: *House, M.D. House* is a medical drama about the tortured brilliant doctor Gregory House, who is more of a detective in the tradition of Sherlock Holmes than anything else. (Get it? Holmes, House.) Each episode features Dr. House and his team trying to diagnose patients with obscure conditions and going to every length (including committing minor crimes) to do so. A recurring storyline is that the patient has gone to multiple doctors who have tried to treat their battery of confusing symptoms using various methods with no success. Finally, the condition becomes life-threatening and Dr. House has to get to the root of the problem to solve the case and save their life.

The reason that House is so successful where all the other doctors fail is that he realizes two things.

First, simply treating the symptoms will never get to the underlying cause. Unless you find the right diagnosis for those symptoms, they're just going to persist and get worse. Sure, you can make the symptoms less annoying, but they're always going to come back until the root cause is found. Bringing this into the parenting world: When we punish or distract our kids to "deal with" the negative behaviors they exhibit rather than addressing the unmet need the behavior communicates, the behaviors we're trying to curtail or prevent are going to keep popping up.

Second, conventional wisdom, standard protocol, and doctors' desire to "do what has always been done" proves ineffective. House would not be House if he did that. He believes you cannot lead with judgment; you have to lead with curiosity, not assuming you know the origin of symptoms. Likewise, parents can't *assume* that what we've been taught about punishment and misbehavior in kids is true. Much of the conventional wisdom given to us by authoritarian ancestors and elders doesn't come from research or neuroscience or psychology; it comes from unquestioned

ideology, illogical reasoning, and unexamined religious beliefs.

Only through curiosity can we find the root cause of what
is ailing those we love and leading to the symptoms we don't
like. Leading with punishment or judgment will never work.

3

What Is Modeled Is Mirrored

Children are great imitators. So give them something
great to imitate.

—UNKNOWN

One of the most unforgettable group coaching experiences I've had with a parent came when a mom brought
to the group a situation that had transpired the previous day.
She was desperate for advice.

That morning her three-year-old son and eight-year-old
daughter had been playing outside on the driveway. Her son
had been drawing on the pavement with sidewalk chalk and
her daughter was just kind of skipping around. Suddenly her
daughter saw a large bug and screamed and jumped backward . . . right onto her little brother's fingers. Thankfully,
there were no broken bones, but there was some skin left on
the driveway and a fair bit of crying.

In the moments following the chaos, before the extent of
the injuries was even known, the mom turned to her daughter
and yelled at her. It wasn't anything outrageous, just something to the effect of: "Why are you reacting like that!? You

know you have to be more careful around your brother! You hurt him!"

Immediately the compassionate little girl started apologizing. She spent the next hour trying to make her brother laugh and feel better. She clearly felt awful and wanted to repair the damage. And that went on for hours, the little girl continuing to feel awful about what had happened long after her little brother was back happily playing.

The mom was bringing this to the group because she was concerned that her daughter was coming down too hard on herself. She felt like it was her fault for yelling in that moment of confusion and fear as she checked to see how badly her son's fingers had been hurt.

I know her fear. My minivan has automatic sliding doors, and two of my three kids have closed those doors onto their own fingers. There is often a terrifying moment between when your child gets hurt and when you know the damage is not severe. Oftentimes we parents lash out in anger when our *real* emotion is fear.

After a pause and some reassurances that any of us might act as she had acted in that moment—with fervent nods of confirmation from fellow parents—I told the story back to her from my perspective.

"You saw your son get hurt and you reacted a little irrationally. Now you're upset with yourself for acting that way. You're beating yourself up for your dysregulation at that moment . . . even though we all can appreciate that we can't control what triggers us. Being scared and lashing out is a quintessentially human thing to do. Is that about right?"

"Yes!" she said. "That's totally it. And now I want to help my daughter to feel better about what happened."

"Right, so now you're looking to undo the harm that your reaction caused."

"Well, I know that I can't undo it, but I can make her feel better about it so she'll stop beating herself up so much."

I saw the glimmers of understanding start around the group. Soon the mom saw it too.

What I had described back to her as her situation perfectly paralleled her daughter's experience:

In a moment of fear and dysregulation, the daughter had acted carelessly and hurt her little brother. Then she spent the rest of the day beating herself up because of the unconscious and almost unavoidable mistake she made when she was afraid.

In a moment of fear and dysregulation, the mom had acted carelessly and hurt her little girl. Now she was, a day later, still beating herself up because of the unconscious and almost unavoidable mistake she made when she was afraid.

I looked at the mom and I told her one of the hardest truths I've had to learn as a parent.

You cannot teach your child what you do not know yourself.

You cannot give to your child that which you cannot give first to yourself.

The first and most important person you have to learn to parent is you.

The Power of Modeling

We all must accept that what we find most challenging about our kids are the same things we most struggle with in *our-*

selves. We're the roots, and the primary way we nurture our kids, whether we like it or not, is not through our interactions with them, but through modeling. This amazing mom was asking her daughter to do something that she was not modeling: extend herself compassion and grace. Until she modeled it, her daughter would be hard-pressed to embody it herself.

Children almost never learn to do the opposite of what is being modeled.

It's easy to think about parenting as something that we *do.* Most parents spend half of their children's formative years away from them doing adult things. Whether the kids are in bed at the end of the night or you're headed off to work after dropping your child off at daycare or school, it's easy to forget sometimes that parenting truly is a 24/7 job.

And it's a 24/7 job because everything you do in life *is* parenting. Whether you're actively engaging your child while taking them to soccer practice or just living your life parallel to them, you are doing the work of parenting.

There is this pressure nowadays to be the perfect parent. I think I know where it comes from. For the first time in human history we are exposed to hundreds of thousands of people on a daily basis . . . and not just their faces on the streets of a busy city or flickering through the light of an old boxy CRT-TV, packed like sardines into a stadium somewhere. We are exposed to people's very *lives* through the power (and perhaps curse) of social media. Right now you can pull out your phone and see a video of me, at home or with my kids, telling you how to do this whole parenting thing better, on TikTok, Instagram, YouTube, or Facebook.

If you care about parenting (which I assume you do since you're reading this book) and a video like that stops your scrolling, the algorithms will undoubtedly feed you another video in the next few minutes telling you how to parent better. Maybe it will be me or it will just be a video of another parent doing something really fun and crafty with their kids.

If you're like the average user who spends about two and a half hours on social media per day, that translates to literally hundreds or even thousands of videos of "perfect" (that is to say "carefully curated") parenting every single week. Compare this experience to that of your mom. She might have spent a couple hours a week with some friends who also had kids. Maybe she was a den mother for Cub Scouts or helped coach your Little League team; a few more hours a week. She saw about 90 percent less than what you see. And what she experienced was people parenting in the *real world* where, try as they might to seem perfect, their flaws inevitably peeked through the cracks. All of their children's behaviors were on full display too, and her other mom friends likely vented about how annoying or difficult their job as a parent was.

The unrealistic standard so many of us now hold ourselves to messes with our brains. It creates unrealistic expectations of what parenting really is. Your flawed and messy parenting in the real world cannot compete with an ideal. Just as pornography messes up people's brains by giving them impossible, unrealistic expectations of sex, and photoshopped Instagram models mess up people's brains by giving them unachievable and unrealistic expectations for their bodies, so too many have come to believe the "perfect parent" myth.[1]

The Problem of Perfectionism

When we attempt to become "perfect" parents and hold ourselves to unrealistic and unachievable standards, we engage in the trap of perfectionism. My definition of parenting perfectionism is loosely based on Brené Brown's definition of perfectionism in her 2010 work *The Gifts of Imperfection*.[2] My definition goes like this:

> Parenting Perfectionism is the pervasive and harmful belief that if you parent perfectly, you will be able to avoid all the hardships that naturally come from being a parent both for yourself and your child.

Perfectionism has an addictive quality to it. You strive to be a perfect parent, eventually falling short because all humans mess up sometimes, and then you beat yourself up for the mistake. This, in turn, leads to self-doubt, low self-esteem, and, according to research, anxiety and depression[3] . . . but because you are a parenting perfectionist you blame these hardships on your own failure to be *perfect*.[4] That inspires you to redouble your efforts and try even harder to be perfect next time, leading to larger emotional and mental consequences when you inevitably fail again.

This was me. I'm *far* from being a perfectionist in most aspects of my life, but as it relates to parenting, I totally am. I was convinced that my parenting mistakes were the source of all of my problems and that by simply not making mistakes, I would solve all of my problems. If my kids were throwing a huge tantrum in the produce section of the grocery store, it must be because I did something wrong as a parent. If my kids weren't sleeping through the night or were wetting the bed, I was somehow to blame. And I know I'm not alone in feeling that way.

I spoke to a parenting influencer and coach not long ago on her podcast. She told me that her team did a poll on one of their posts that got a huge response. The two questions were, "How many of you think that it's possible to be a perfect parent?" and "If you could be a perfect parent, would all of your parenting struggles go away?" According to her, the results were shocking. More than 90 percent of parents believed that perfect parenting was obtainable, and 98 percent believed that if they could become a perfect parent, their parenting issues would go away.

But it's not true! This is the trap of parenting perfectionism. The harder you try to be perfect, the greater the consequences. In fact, people who continue down this path to its most extreme end can wind up with suicidal ideations.[5]

And if that's not motivation enough to drop the ideal, consider that we are also passing this harmful worldview on to our kids. . . .

The overwhelming majority of what our kids learn from us comes not from our perfectly scripted conversations with them, and certainly not through our punishments, but through *modeling*.

You've heard the adage "Monkey see, monkey do." It's true. Humans are basically just really smart, really social, mostly bald monkeys. A massive amount of children's social emotional learning is achieved through observation. Our kids, especially really young kids, are little mimics. They see how we interact with the world around us, how we cope with disappointment, how we process through our feelings, and how we relate to our partner and other humans, and they mimic.

That's why our mistakes *can* become such powerful parenting moments. If we recover and process well, they get to learn how to recover and process well too.

The mechanism in their brain responsible for this "monkey see, monkey do" phenomenon are tiny neurons called "mirror neurons," which I'll explain in a moment. For now, it's enough to understand that observation is one of the primary ways our brains learn how to do things.

Long before scientists knew about mirror neurons, the neuro-mechanism for observational learning and cognitive development, we already knew how they worked in kids. Way back in 1961, Albert Bandura conducted the now famous "Bobo doll experiment."[6] He gathered seventy-two preschool children and divided them into three main groups each containing twelve boys and twelve girls.

- The first group of twenty-four watched adults, of both their gender and the opposite gender, attack the "Bobo doll" aggressively.
- The second group of twenty-four watched adults, again of both their gender and the opposite gender, model peaceful, specifically nonaggressive play.
- The third group of twenty-four was exposed to no modeling at all.

Results showed what you might expect. Children exposed to adults acting aggressively imitated their aggression when later placed in a new environment without the adults. Interestingly, boys tended to imitate aggression more than girls did, especially when the model was male and exhibited a socially typical masculine aggression.

Children (both boys and girls) who viewed nonaggressive adults, particularly the subdued male, were generally less aggressive than even the control group who had no modeling at all. Monkey see, monkey do. What we didn't know in 1961 is that mirror neurons are responsible for this phenomenon. In just the last decade or so, fMRI scans have begun to reveal how mirror neurons work. But to understand how mirror neurons work, you first need to understand how regular old neurons work.

Imagine your brain as a library of information. Instead of books, your brain is filled with billions and billions of neurons. These neurons, much like books, are like little packets of information. You have neurons for hamburgers and oak trees and even neurons for sensory experiences like that lurch in the pit of your stomach when you're falling backward and you can't stop yourself. When you are presented with a picture of a hamburger—or the smell of one wafting down an alley from that dive metal bar on the North Side of Chicago—the neurons for *hamburger* light up with tiny electrical pulses.

But the neurons for hamburger aren't the only neurons to fire. Chances are, a bunch of other neurons are going to fire too. Things associated with hamburgers. Milkshakes and French fries, and, if you've had the misfortune of eating a hamburger right before you got sick, maybe the neurons for feeling like you're going to puke.

These related neurons fire because of what neuroscientists call "Hebb's law." Hebb's law states that "any two cells or systems of cells that are repeatedly active at the same time will tend to become 'associated,' so that activity in *one* facilitates activity in the *other*."[7] More commonly, you'll hear Hebb's law cited with the simple and memorable turn of phrase, "*Neurons that fire together, wire together.*" Your brain is a huge collection of neurons all linked together in massive, constantly changing webs. It's all very mind-blowing.

Blazing a New Trail

Let's use learning the guitar as an example. The learning curve for guitar, as anyone who has tried to learn any musical instrument will tell you, is pretty steep. You try to force your fingers into these awkward, often painful shapes to form chords all while trying to do something entirely different with your other hand—strumming—to generate sound. If you start on brass strings like I did, the pain isn't just limited to the cramping in your left hand. Your fingers burn, too, until the tiny blisters on the tips of your fingers become calluses over time. It can take months or even years to feel competent.

As you practice the same chords over and over, neurons in your brain responsible for the shape, pressure, and feeling of your individual fingers on the strings fire in the same succession over and over until their firing becomes linked in a neural web. They, in other words, "wire together."

Every guitar player who has played long enough has experienced this phenomenon in action. One day you stop thinking *middle finger third fret E string, index second fret A string, ring finger third fret B string, pinky third fret E string* and instead just think *G major.* That's the magic of our brains. Our neurons become linked and fire all together.

These connections between neurons are called *neural pathways.* Think of neural pathways as paths through the woods of the brain. When you first try to blaze a new trail through a wooded area it is difficult and can even be painful. The brush is thick, and you'll have to cut it back and stamp it down before the path is even visible. Each time you walk down that path, it gets a little clearer until the vines aren't entangling you and you don't have to duck under branches anymore.

This is how neural pathways are built too. The initial path can be difficult to establish, but eventually it becomes almost entirely automatic. You won't look at a G on a chord chart and accidentally play a B anymore. G has become linked with the feeling of your fingers on the strings in the shape of a G and even the sound of the G chord bouncing around simultaneously in *both* your prefrontal cortex and your limbic system (yes, music is crazy). The path has been cemented.

The Brain's Mirroring Mechanism

Mirror neurons are neurons that fire *not only* when you do a thing yourself, but when you see someone else doing that thing. For example, if you are our hypothetical guitar student, simply watching someone else play a G chord will activate mirror neurons in your brain, reinforcing the neural pathway. This is why watching a professional basketball player with a perfect jump shot (Klay Thompson, for the NBA fans out there) can actually make you a better jump shooter yourself, even while you're sitting on the couch. It's also likely a factor contributing to why studies show that children who are read to on a regular basis, all things being equal, usually learn how to read faster and with more ease.

If you want to see mirror neurons at work out in the real world, I invite you to act as an undercover neuroscientist at the next available adult social function. I admit, for some of us with young kids, you might have to wait quite a while. But even if it's next Thanksgiving, try to remember this and try it out.

Once the conversation is in full swing and everyone is relatively relaxed, take a drink of water. Then glance around the table. Chances are at least one other person, if not several people, will unconsciously reach for their glass too. Your conscious act of drinking water just caused them to *unconsciously* fire their mirror neurons.

Fun party trick. Clue your partner into the gag—heck, tell everyone at the party. It won't matter. If they're sufficiently distracted they'll still reach for the glass. In fact, even though I know about this stuff and am usually on the lookout for it, I can't help but open my own mouth when I hold a spoon up to feed one of my kids. That's the power of mirror neurons.

As you perform the same actions over and over in front of your kids (or even in their periphery), their mirror neurons are firing, blazing new neural pathways in their brain that will become *their* factory-default conditioning. If you model being rude or aggressive to your partner, they'll begin to develop neural pathways consistent with that modeling first in their childhood relationships, and later in their adult relationships. If you model calm, compassionate, and empathetic respect for others, they will build neural networks consistent with *those* values.

So what would you guess will happen when your kids see *you* modeling emotional regulation?

Kids may lack the brain development to regulate overwhelming emotions independently, but they don't lack mirror neurons. If you demonstrate how to regulate down and ground yourself when you're about to lose it, they can and will get practice by proximity. This means that you can effectively leverage your own ability to self-regulate to help them build those pathways for de-escalation before their brain is independently able to do it.

I get it if you're skeptical. It doesn't seem like your emotional regulation is making much of a difference when your three-year-old is screaming at the top of their lungs because you accidentally picked the wrong-shaped pasta at dinner. But their proximity to you, an adult who is responding calmly and intentionally, is slowly forming the neural pathways for self-control for the rest of their lives.

This is so incredibly important for parents to understand because we mistakenly operate so frequently from the "do as I say, not as I do" philosophy on life. We think that the way to instill values, positive relationship dynamics, or even morality is through communicating those values verbally and often through punishment. This is wrong. Children are far more influenced by what we do than by what we say. Our actions, more than our words, lay the foundation of values, positive relationships, and morality in their lives. As parents, *embodying* our ideals is far more powerful than preaching them. We teach by example, not just through instruction.

This is why the first person you need to learn to parent is always you. Not only will you have far better life satisfaction and emotional regulation when you align your life with your stated values, but you will also be a far more effective parent and communicator.

They're Learning How to Be a Person

Think of it this way. If you started a new job and, as part of your training, you had to shadow your manager or a more seasoned employee as they performed the tasks you would soon be responsible for, it would be incredibly confusing if, in one breath, they told you how to do those tasks with specific instructions, and then proceeded to do those tasks completely differently as you observed. All of the data your senses were taking in as observational learning would be running counter to the instructions being given. Which do you think you would be more likely to do? Follow the verbal instructions or mirror what you observed?

It shouldn't surprise you that, without intense cognitive effort—beyond the capacity of a young child's underdeveloped brain—mirroring would almost certainly be the way you would go. In fact, even if you were able to force yourself to "do as they said, not as they did" until you had done the task enough times to build up the required neural pathways, you would likely lapse back into what you had observed rather than what you had been instructed to do as soon as you stopped paying close enough attention.

This is why, if you want your child to behave in a certain way or embody certain values for greater life flourishing, you have to learn *first* to embody those values with some measure of consistency for yourself. If you fail to do so, your actions and therefore their observational learning will always be working *against* your parenting. This is the very definition of parenting *harder* rather than *smarter*.

Your personal daily battles literally shape your children's futures. If you endure a toxic workplace and a bullying boss, silenced by unaddressed childhood tendencies to please others, your children are likely silently learning to accept the same abuse. Despite your words of caution, they will reflect the relational patterns you embody—both the good and the bad. Your actions speak the lessons they'll carry into their adult lives.

The same is true for toxic romantic relationships. There is a lot of scientific research into why people who come from violent homes so often become abusers or victims of abuse themselves. While every case is different, the numbers bear out that what was modeled during childhood is mirrored in adulthood, even when it is so clearly against the best interests of everyone involved.

Similarly, if you are your own worst critic, failing to extend yourself grace, compassion, or understanding when you make mistakes or are dysregulated and aren't at your best, your children will learn to do the same when they make mistakes or aren't at their best.

If, on the other hand, you realize that mistakes are one of the primary ways we learn and grow and that beating ourselves up about them does absolutely no good, your kids will learn to model that mindset.

If you're wondering why I'm using this "inner critic" example as the main example in this chapter rather than abuse or some other issue, it's because this is one of my major parenting struggles. The reason I could detect this so easily in my group coaching environment was that this was one of the behaviors modeled to me in my childhood. My dad, and his father before him, was his own worst critic when he made mistakes. I am my own worst critic when I make mistakes. My oldest is now his own worst critic when he makes mistakes . . . but we're trying to learn and practice compassion.

It is because of this foundational parenting principle—that our children mirror what we model—that we get trendy phrases like "cycle breakers." A cycle breaker is a person who does the self-work and introspective reflection to eventually make the intentional, conscious decision to do things differently from how they were modeled. This sometimes requires or is helped along by a therapist and always includes intentional contemplative practice. It's a *ton* of work, but it's work that pays off.

If you are a parent who is going punishment-free and that's

not how your parents (or your grandparents, great-grandparents, and so on) did it, congratulations, you're on your way to becoming a cycle breaker.

Cycle Breakers: Breaking Generational Curses

Some old church ladies I know like to call this "breaking generational curses." Cycle breakers create change not just for themselves but for their children and their entire family for generations to come. They break the cycle of destructive modeling and mirroring passed down from parent to child for countless generations.

To illustrate this principle in my master's program, one of the counseling faculty had everyone do a genogram. A genogram is a way of mapping your family of origin's relational data. Where a family tree will only show genetic links, the genogram illustrates common issues like divorce, suicide, separation, and premature death. Each of these unique problems is given a distinct symbol, and by mapping a family back two or more generations, a person can see patterns of dysfunction appear.

I highly recommend making a genogram of your own family. Although, be careful asking relatives about these things. Depending on family culture, you may have a hard time filling out your genogram. It's like the hit Disney song "We Don't Talk About Bruno" from the movie *Encanto*. In many families, dysfunction is hidden and masked, and you may learn about a lot of skeletons when you try to fill out your genogram.

I'll be the first to tell you, looking at your genogram is an eye-opening experience. Suddenly you realize that so many of the problems you and your nuclear family faced in your childhood were directly linked to things like hereditary mental illness and generational cycles of mirroring and modeling. In one stroke you realize that even though it didn't start with you, it very well could end with you. And as daunting as it may seem, it's also incredibly empowering.

After all, that's the ultimate goal, isn't it? To give our kids a better life and more tools than we had? In order to do that, we're going to have to deal with *ourselves*.

Even though mirror neurons might be behind some harmful generational cycles, they can also be one of our greatest assets. In fact, you can capitalize on them using the same principle as the "dinner table water drinking" party trick I explained earlier.

Next time your child is having a meltdown or tantrum, don't try to talk them out of it. When they're in this brain state they're usually pretty nonreceptive to language since their prefrontal cortex, the part of their brain you can reason with, is basically offline. Simply meet them at their level, eye to eye, and proceed to relax each part of your upper body. Let your shoulders roll back and sag, let your arms go limp, and rest comfortably. Relax your hands, dislodge your tongue from the roof of your mouth, and—keeping your lips just the slightest bit open—slightly relax your jaw. Finally, close your eyes and take three deep breaths in through your nose and out through your mouth, exhaling longer than you inhale.

Breathing these centering breaths is scientifically proven to help humans move out of their limbic system and back into their prefrontal cortex. You'll be able to respond to your kids' dysfunction and co-regulate them out of it rather than reacting and driving them deeper into the dysregulation.[8]

These breaths will not only make you a thousand times more ready to engage your kids effectively, but the breaths will also help *them* calm down. As you model the breaths, their mirror neurons will fire and, if they don't intentionally resist the urge, they will begin to slowly mirror you, which stimulates their *vagus nerve* and calms them down almost instantly. This process is perhaps one of the simplest and yet most powerful parenting "brain hacks" I know. And it works by leveraging the power of mirror neurons.

4

Using Consequences Effectively

In nature there are neither rewards nor punishments;
there are consequences.

—ROBERT GREEN INGERSOLL

A few years ago I built a deck over our patio. It was a ton of work and exhausting, but for me, working on projects like that is incredibly cathartic. Apart from getting to work outside in comfortable spring weather for several days and the satisfaction that comes from building something with your hands, the best part of big projects like these is that I often get to work with my kids. In this case, my helper was my oldest son, who was five at the time.

We carefully built the frame and then had a thousand dollars' worth of 16-to-20-foot fresh-treated, 5/4-thick decking dropped on the driveway. I methodically sorted the decking so that when laid on the frame and screwed in, the finished product would be straight, clean, smooth, and altogether gorgeous.

My dad had our deck built the year before I was born, and I grew up for eighteen years watching him carefully wash, stain, and seal it every fall on one of his few work-free Saturdays. My family loved that deck. We played on it for hours as kids, and on almost every summer weekend evening my parents would fill the table on the deck with pork chops and burgers and farm-fresh corn on the cob soaked in butter and salt. There we would sit for hours into the evening telling stories, laughing, and getting eaten alive by mosquitoes who were undeterred by the latest new-age method of repellant my mom had heard about on NPR.

I had all those same hopes for our new deck in a house that was finally feeling like our forever home after two-plus years of hard sweat equity.

Imagine my surprise when I walked out to see my son putting the finishing touches on a bright red Sharpie racetrack, the perfect size for Matchbox cars, drawn on that beautiful brand-new deck.

My son looked at me and I looked at him and his face changed as he realized that what he had just done was not even remotely appreciated.

In that moment I did something that, to this day, I don't know how I managed. I yelled his name to get him to stop but then I stopped talking. *I resisted the urge to punish.* Maybe I was just in shock or maybe it had something to do with working with him for the last week on the deck, but I didn't grab him or march him into the house to put him in a time-out. I didn't start to hurl threats at him. I didn't scream him into a puddle about how he just ruined something that we had saved up for and dreamed about. I walked over to him, mouth clenched shut, pocketed the red Sharpie so he couldn't keep drawing, and walked away.

Looking back, it was one of my best parenting moments. Sure, it doesn't *feel* Instagram-worthy to post about what you didn't do, but it was the best thing I could have done at that moment.

Let me explain.

When I look at all the questions I get from parents trying to go punishment-free out in the world, by far the most common way they start is, "What do I do when . . ."

Sometimes it's, "What do I do when my three-year-old pushes her little sister to the ground?" Or, "What do I do when my seven-year-old refuses to get off his iPad?" Or, "What do I do when my eighteen-month-old bites me?" They're all good questions with no easy or obvious answers. But they all betray belief in a fundamental assumption in discipline and parenting: When a child acts out, their parents should intervene and do *something* in the moment. For authoritarian parents, that something is usually punishment. But what about for the rest of us? Surely we can't just do nothing, right?

This instinct to "do something" shouldn't surprise us. For one, it's how most of us were raised. Punishment followed misbehavior usually before the dust had even settled. (I remember one such time in my childhood where I was shamed and grounded literally while the soda cans I was hurling from the deck were still hissing ominously out of their new dents and perforations. We liked how they were exploding when they landed. . . .)

The parents of past generations I've talked to like to call this parenting technique "nipping it in the bud." The thinking goes, if you punish quickly (and severely) enough, your child will link the punishment to the action in such a way that they will remember the punishment before acting out the next time. . . . If you don't, they won't remember what they did.

Adults often mistakenly equate their inability to remember

things that happened during their childhood twenty years ago with children having bad memory generally. The latter is just not true. Ask my seven-year-old about Minecraft or my three-year-old about *PAW Patrol* and you'll realize their memories are as robust as those of most adults. Yet not long ago, I was at lunch with a man in his eighties who had raised multiple kids to adulthood. When the topic of disciplining children came up, he told me with all the confidence in the world that kids can't usually remember anything that happens to them so you have to discipline them the moment you catch them misbehaving. I expressed some hesitation, but he waved it off.

"You're thinking of them like they're adults. They're more like dogs. You can't discipline a dog for peeing on the carpet a few hours later; you have to stop them while they're doing it!"

I want to pause for a moment here and point out that, as crazy as that might sound reading it in a book, this man was not saying anything that most parents do not suggest through their actions. Most parents I know attempt to teach their children far more like they are dogs—with yelling, harsh punishment, or exaggerated disappointment in the moment—than how they would teach a new coworker who had just filled out the expense report completely wrong.

That's why, when we talk about consequences, we're not just talking about *how* to discipline, we're also talking about *when* to discipline.

Consequences vs. Punishment

Consequences and *punishment* are not the same thing, even if the words are used interchangeably in Western parenting.

For example, I remember my parents and my friends' parents euphemistically using the word *consequences* when what they really meant was *punishment*. They might say something like, "If you don't stop doing that right now, you're going to have a consequence." But ultimately, to use the word in that way—the way so many parents still use the word today—is a stretch . . . at best.

So then what are consequences? How are parents supposed to use consequences effectively? How can a book called *Punishment-Free Parenting* possibly be advocating for the use of . . . consequences?

One of the most common questions I get from parents is "How do I use consequences the 'right' way?"

First off, we need to adopt a somewhat neutral view of the word *consequences*. There can be good or bad consequences; in fact, there can be consequences that are neither good nor bad. Consequences are simply the outcomes of our actions. The consequence of being kind and friendly to the other kids at the park will probably be making friends. The consequence of being mean and exclusionary will be not making friends.

Unlike punishment, consequences *are* one of the most impactful and effective ways kids learn.

I'll give you an example from my college years. I have always had a good memory—so good that I rarely had to take notes at school. Throughout my entire K–12 education and even my first two years in college, as long as I was present and attentive during the lecture, I could almost always regurgitate the relevant information at test time without ever taking notes or extensively studying. If this annoys you, don't worry. This story is about consequences.

My junior year I transferred schools to play volleyball at a tiny college in rural South Carolina. Most of my credits transferred without issue, but I still had to take a couple of freshman-level classes that were requirements at the new school and had no analogue at my previous university.

As you can imagine, coming from an impressive Chicago suburban high school and having made it through two years of university already with a solid GPA to show for it, I didn't think much of having to take "World Civilizations Prior to 1600" with a bunch of eighteen-year-olds at some rural college. Dr. Farmer, the professor, encouraged us to write down everything he wrote on the board. But as I sat through the first two lectures, I realized that most of what he wrote down I would definitely remember apart from some trivial details—the spellings of names and the estimated dates of conquests or the precise geographic locations of ancient cities and waterways. Details like that never seem to be relevant to actually *understanding* those civilizations or their importance in world history. The important stuff, I didn't need to write down. I could hold it all in my head.

I sat through five weeks of lectures with a notepad in front of me that I doodled on for show. When the first test came, about ancient Mesopotamia, I figured I did pretty well. I was able to demonstrate that I understood their culture's key advancements and why ancient Mesopotamia was relevant to historians. I even knew some important names. Sure, I wasn't super clear on the spelling of those names or the estimated dates those people had lived, nor was I able to plot the precise locations of the archeological dig sites on a map. But what did those trivial things matter to me? I had Google for those types of questions. I remembered the important stuff.

Well, it mattered, as it turned out, a lot to Dr. Farmer. He had a memory that made mine look like a goldfish's, and to him, the ability to regurgitate dates, correctly spell names, and plot ancient and modern cities precisely on a blank map was *exactly* the way to demonstrate you knew anything about that civilization.

I got my test paper back with a big red shiny *D* on it. I was shocked, but that was the consequence of arrogantly refusing to take notes or study. As it turned out, if I wanted to ace this class full of freshmen led by a professor barely five years older than me, I was going to have to take notes and study hard the things that mattered to him. You better believe that consequence inspired a change in my behavior.

According to research, after modeling, it is mistakes and failures—that is, actions, intended or unintended, with undesirable consequences—that are the primary ways humans learn. Mistakes are also one of the biggest confidence builders, and we'll get into that later on in the book.

What research says specifically is that mistakes lead us to understand the world more deeply and that memories that include mistakes tend to be better retained and are more accessible to help us make different choices in the future.[1] In fact, some studies on education seem to indicate that direct instruction is actually *less* effective than allowing a person to learn from failure.[2] In short, letting someone fail at something is often a *better* way to teach them than telling them the "right" way to do it in the first place.

Think about the implications of this for our kids. How often do we insist on drilling into our kids the "right" way to do a thing? How often do we preempt their mistakes and save them from certain failure? How often do we intervene unnecessarily and actually inhibit learning?

In numerous studies on how people learn, it's been shown that having participants take a test before teaching them directly, grading that test, and then allowing them to learn from their mistakes is far more effective than direct instruction at the outset. This is because the mistakes themselves often inspire us to learn.[3]

Timing Is Everything

Let's take it back to the red Sharpie on the new deck.

I ended that story by saying I walked away with the marker, but that was only the end of that part of the story. I walked away because, at that moment, my son was not in a receptive space for teaching and I was not in a place to teach. Dysregulated brains—when our amygdala starts driving and we go into survival mode—are not primed for learning or instruction. By stepping away before I engaged, I allowed both of us enough time to regulate and be in a good teaching and learning brain space.

Had I followed the conventional parenting wisdom that demands we engage our kids directly at the moment of dysfunction, I would have been fighting a futile battle; trying to force a child to learn when he was in an anti-learning space.

Here's how to remember this the next time you're in a situation with a dysregulated child:

Don't fight with lizards.

Remember when I pointed out in chapter 1 that children in "survival mode" are being run by their "lizard brain"? Can you imagine trying to argue or force logic upon a bearded dragon? It would be pointless. That's what it's like trying to fight, argue, or even discipline a dysregulated kid.

So what happened with my son and the marker?

Well, as I said, by some miracle I walked away in the moment after procuring our deck's murder weapon and mitigating future damage. Then I cooled off enough to get *curious rather than furious*. That's when I realized some of the following things:

- There was no way, based on the look on his face, that my son had any clue what he was doing. He was like me with the soda cans. I needed to find out more about how he could have had this lapse in understanding.
- Only one person in our house uses Sharpies. Me. I had been using that particular red Sharpie to mark deck measurements, and—as I have a particularly bad habit of doing with most of my tools, to my wife's absolute dismay—I had likely left it lying out exactly where I had been using it . . . on the deck.
- Of all the tools I left out, including a charged air compressor and a plugged-in circular saw, the one that was least likely to get my son killed was the red Sharpie. If I'm being honest, I was insanely lucky that I had a damaged deck and not a hurt kid.

Who was to blame for the marker on the deck? Well, honestly, both of us. I was to blame because I hadn't kept dangerous and damaging things away from a five-year-old, nor had I taught him how to use the thing I left in his domain. He was to blame because he still colored on the deck without asking, and we needed to prevent that from happening again.

Before we talked about consequences (but after we were both in a regulated place), we sat down and had a conversation about the deck. I asked my son what questions he had, and he wound up asking several clarifying questions that, if the "discipline" had been me screaming at him in the moment, would have probably gone unanswered and bitten me down the road.

He asked, "Is it OK to draw on the deck with other things that are erasable, like pencils?"

"Nope," I said.

"Is it OK to draw on other things that aren't wood with a Sharpie?"

"Like what?"

"The garage," he said. "It's made of concrete."

I shook my head. "No. We can't draw on the garage in Sharpie either. In fact, now that I'm thinking about it, we shouldn't use Sharpie without a grown-up until we're a little older."

"How do I know which markers are Sharpies?"

I showed him the logo. "If you see one like this around," I said, "bring it to me and I'll put it away immediately. You don't want one of your brothers getting these either. I'll try to find a place where I can keep them so I stop leaving them around."

This is the power of being curious rather than furious, of leading with *connection* instead of correction.

The discipline wasn't just limited to a conversation either. It also included a *consequence*. Specifically, my son had to help me get the red marker off the deck. We did that with sandpaper and sweat.

As we took turns with the sandpaper, slowly erasing the red marker, I told him about *The Karate Kid* where Daniel LaRusso had to sand Mr. Miyagi's deck to learn karate. It was a bonding experience and educational, but it certainly wasn't easy. He complained that he had to fix the problem he had caused, and I had to hold the boundary until we finished. He learned that day the actual lived consequences of his indiscretion with the red Sharpie. We had to repair together what was damaged.

The problem is, most parents I know conflate this type of consequence with other ineffective punishments and just assume they're the same. Consider how it differs from punishments like taking away a child's tablet for a week, putting them in time-out, or using physical violence. None of those things express to the child *why* what they did is an issue; they only express *that* you are upset. The *why* is left up to the child—and more often than not, they fill in that blank incorrectly.

Here are some common *whys* my own kids have come up with—adapted for this example—when we fail to communicate effectively:

- My dad doesn't like that I picked the color red or that I drew a racetrack instead of something else.
- I'm not allowed to draw on wood stuff (which might be partially true but is incomplete).
- Sharpies are bad (again, incomplete).
- Dad is just mean about some stuff.
- I am naughty or bad.
- I have no idea why what I did was wrong but I'm afraid of Dad now.

On the other hand, my son absolutely knows now why we don't draw on decks with a Sharpie. A Sharpie is not a washable marker, and to get it off, you're going to have to sand for a while. He learned his lesson not because I was a tyrant who forced him into a punishment, but because he was allowed to experience the outcomes of his actions with me by his side.

Learning from failure is so effective because it works *with* the way that our brain naturally processes information instead of *against* it.

Natural vs. Logical Consequences

The human brain is, fundamentally, a connection-making machine. It is constantly trying to draw connections between things. But brains are also *really* lazy. By that I mean, they take a lot of shortcuts called heuristics. They have to. They already use up about 25 percent of our energy. If they didn't take shortcuts, we would be in serious trouble.

When we send our child into their limbic system by shouting, punishing harshly, or physically hurting them, they draw comparatively fewer connections—and the shortcuts their brain takes to draw them have the potential to leave them with the wrong answer.

But even when the discipline we employ doesn't send them into fight or flight, if it's not explicitly related to the action they took, they're *still* likely to misunderstand our motivations for their punishment. This becomes, of course, less true the older they grow. Teenagers have a much greater ability to draw the connections necessary even when the behavior and consequence are less related. But especially when kids are under the age of ten, the best practice is to make sure any consequence that you use is explicitly and directly connected to what they did.

A lot of people think that what I've described so far is an example of natural consequence, but actually, it's an example of what parenting experts like Aliza Pressman call "logical consequences."[4] A truly natural consequence occurs when the parent steps aside and allows the natural outcome of a child's actions to occur. If a child refuses to put on their coat when it's cold out, and the parent doesn't intervene, the child will be cold. Cause and effect.

Here are some examples of natural consequences that are usually effective:

- Your child refuses to put on a coat, so you allow them to experience being cold while keeping the coat with you. Once they experience the temperature, they can choose to put on the coat.
- Your child hurts another child at the park, and as a result, that child does not want to play anymore.
- Your child does not do their homework and gets a poor grade.
- Your child does not put their favorite sweatshirt in the hamper and so it doesn't get washed and it's unavailable for them to wear the next day.
- Your child procrastinates at bedtime and so you run out of time for a story.

The key with all of these things is that you, as the parent, are *only* intervening to direct your child's conscious attention to the natural outcomes of their actions. In order to do this effectively, you have to be willing to let them face those consequences. If you, in the end, give in and read a story anyway, the consequence is not internalized. For this reason, a lot of self-described "gentle parents" really struggle with holding boundaries firmly enough to employ natural consequences effectively. We all love our kids, and it's hard to let them face the music sometimes. When we consistently fail to allow our children to face consequences, we become *permissive* parents, and our kids tend to suffer more in the long term as a result.

While I like a lot of natural consequences, I've also seen parents take them too far. They use natural consequences, in effect, as license to allow their child to experience disproportionate levels of harm. This is punishment and it can even be dangerous.

For example, I've heard parents say that the natural consequence for forgetting your water bottle at home is that you are thirsty. That might be a fine natural consequence for a walk around the neighborhood in the fall. If, on the other hand, it is a 90-degree day and your child is at a sporting event, that natural consequence is both disproportionate and dangerous. Any natural consequence that leads to real potential danger—beyond being unethical—will inevitably trigger your child's survival brain to take over and any learning will be lost.

I get it; sometimes parents can get carried away and feel like they *have* to hold the boundary at all costs, but we need to know when to stop.

Most of these should go without saying, and this is by no means an exhaustive list, but here are some examples of natural consequences that are disproportionate:

- Allowing your child to get dehydrated or sick to prove a point.
- Allowing your child to get hypothermic.
- Hitting or biting your child when they hit or bite you (because that is what would happen if they did that to their peers).

- Allowing your child to stay up the entire night so they will "feel it tomorrow."
- Allowing your child to get any severe physical injury.

Your job as a parent is to know the difference between natural consequences that might be mildly uncomfortable and lead to change, and those that are dangerous. When you deem that one is dangerous, you intervene. When you deem that one is only uncomfortable, you can opt to allow your child to face that consequence and then process with them later, again, directing their conscious attention to the natural outcome of their choices and behavior.

When a natural consequence doesn't make sense, then you can use a *logical* consequence instead. The difference between a natural consequence and a logical consequence is that the parent is not simply stepping aside and allowing the consequence to play out, but rather is intervening by imposing a consequence to solidify the teaching.

The consequence of having my son help me sand the deck was a *logical* one. He didn't care, and in fact preferred that the deck had red marker on it, and so the simple existence of red marker on the deck wasn't going to be an effective natural consequence. So because there was no obvious natural consequence, the sanding was a consequence imposed by me, his dad, in order to help him understand why the thing he did was not ideal and what it would take to fix it.

This is a variation on the most common logical consequence—having a child clean up the mess they made. I will usually help my kids clean up their messes (as I helped him sand the deck) because it has the dual benefit of instilling the value of helping others and getting it done more efficiently, but I wouldn't do it *for* them. If the solution or cleanup is something the child simply cannot do (like unclogging the toilet they shoved half a roll of toilet paper down, like my two-year-old did last week), at least have them sit with you while you do it.

I could list dozens of examples of logical consequences— from having your child pay for something they broke to temporarily restricting access to a tablet when your child is using it inappropriately—but instead of doing that, I'm going to walk you through an acronym I developed for parents that helps determine how to use effective consequences. The acronym is WRAP.

Logical Consequences: The WRAP Acronym

W—Warranted

The *W* in WRAP stands for *warranted*—and we always have to begin here because, in more than 90 percent of cases, an additional logical consequence is unnecessary and therefore not warranted.

The question is always, what is the best way for my child to learn; *not* what can I do to my child in order to make myself feel better. The latter is a punishment mindset.

Logical consequences, in my experience, tend to be less effective than natural consequences and are therefore counterproductive if your child is already experiencing the natural consequences of their actions. The consequence of not studying and getting a bad grade was a *natural* consequence for me in college. No one did it *to* me; it was just the natural outcome of my decisions. It happened and I learned from it. If I had been additionally punished via a *logical* consequence, that natural learning would have actually been obscured.

To explain what I mean by this, let's take a classic sibling example where many parents think a logical consequence is warranted . . . but, in my opinion, it's not. An older child pushes their little brother to the ground while roughhousing and causes their brother to get hurt. Ideally, you first intervene to comfort the *hurt* child with empathy and validate their experience and only then turn your attention to the older sibling.

But often that's not how we respond. Many parents, in this situation, get caught up in emotions and actually round on the aggressor first, which ultimately sends the wrong message. They put the older child in time-out, threaten to take away a prized possession like an electronic device, or even threaten to hurt the older child in retaliation.

But is a consequence even necessary and warranted? Well, it depends. I would argue, at least with kids who are generally kind and empathetic—that is, kids for whom kindness and empathy have been modeled by a loving and attentive caregiver—probably not.

The consequence was a natural one. Their brother got hurt. If anything, your job at that moment is to make space for the older child to come to terms with that consequence and consider the more lasting consequences to their relationship. I might say something to the effect of, "We can't play rough if we can't respect boundaries," or "I don't think your little brother is going to like playing like that if it goes too far and he gets hurt."

Statements like those are designed to draw your child's attention to their actions and the natural consequences of those actions. If your child is already experiencing a natural consequence, adding on a logical consequence (or especially a punishment) is only likely to confuse the real-world outcomes of continuing to behave in that problematic way.

R—Reasonable

The *R* in WRAP stands for *reasonable*. Are you and your child being reasonable when you're about to give a consequence? If not, stop and wait until you are.

When it comes to giving a consequence—once you deem one is warranted—you need to make sure that you are in a reasonable, rational, and generally calm headspace. If you are all up in your feelings, being driven by your amygdala, you're not going to be reasonable, and the consequences are almost always going to be ineffective or in some way miscommunicated.

In fact, I don't know if I've ever encountered a parent who was totally out of control and yet still able to give an effective logical consequence (that wasn't actually just a punishment).

Often, after stopping short of doling out what you felt was a warranted consequence in your triggered state, you'll realize that a consequence is not even warranted. I can't tell you the number of times that's been my experience. It sure seems to me that every consequence or punishment, no matter how severe, and no matter how bad the child already feels, is warranted when I'm in rage mode and not being reasonable.

And remember that you're not the only one who needs to be in a rational headspace before imposing consequences. Teaching a dysregulated brain is like trying to argue with a lizard: totally fruitless. This goes for processing through conversations and giving logical consequences. It may feel like you're letting them "get away with" the problematic behavior when you don't throw out a consequence in the moment, but you're not. It's way more effective to wait until everyone is *reasonable* to proceed.

A—Associated

The *A* in WRAP stands for *associated*. Is the logical consequence you're deploying associated with the behavior you're trying to limit or encourage? If not, there's a high likelihood that it's going to be ineffective at best, and at worst, totally misconstrued and pointless.

If, in our roughhousing example above, you determined that a logical consequence was warranted and you and your child were in a reasonable state, utilizing a consequence like "They cannot have ice cream for dessert" or "No Minecraft for a week" is likely to be confusing and ineffective. On the other hand, using a logical *associated* consequence like "We can't play this game for the rest of the day. We need to take a break until we find a way to do it safely" might be *highly* effective.

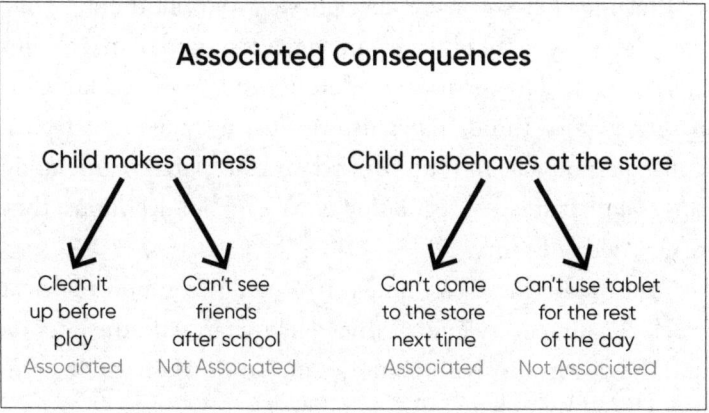

Associated Consequences

Child makes a mess

Clean it up before play
Associated

Can't see friends after school
Not Associated

Child misbehaves at the store

Can't come to the store next time
Associated

Can't use tablet for the rest of the day
Not Associated

One problem with the majority of disciplinary strategies is that parents fail to associate the discipline with behavior that

needs to be modified. Many parents respond that this is easier said than done. That they "can't think of an *associated* consequence in the moment" and that it's "unreasonable to expect
them to be able to." They're right. That's why we step back
and pause before we go through the WRAP framework. It is
going to take creative problem solving and collaboration *with*
your kids to come up with effective consequences.

By ensuring that our logical consequences are *associated*
with the behaviors and outcomes that led to them, we work
with our kid's brain and memory systems instead of against
them.

P—Proportional

The *P* in WRAP stands for *proportional*. A logical consequence, in order to be effective, has to be proportionate to the
harm caused. When logical consequences are disproportionate to the behavior they are addressing, they cease to be effective and usually become punishments.

Imagine that you were an eight-year-old child and, while
your parent was out of the room, you attempted to make yourself a snack. The result was a kitchen that looked like a tor-
nado had gone through it. This is a clear instance for a logical
consequence: Clean it up. But when your parent came upon
this scene, instead of regulating down and being curious, they
responded with fury.

"You made this mess, and you're going to spend the next
week cleaning every inch of this house. Start with the kitchen
and the downstairs bathroom. Let me know when you're done
and I'll tell you what you're doing next."

What would your eight-year-old brain learn from this experience? "When I make a mess while I'm getting a snack, I

need to clean it up," or "Dad is irrational and made me clean for hours over basically nothing; I better tread lightly around him"?

Or, if it's hard to take on the perspective of your own eight-year-old self, just think about how you prefer to have mistakes addressed at work as an adult. When you give your boss a report that is missing vital information, would you respond better to . . .

"Hey, it looks like some of the information we need was left off the report. We've gotta redo the report with that included. Do you need help finding that information or anything else to make that happen?"

Or . . .

"Hey, you forgot the most important part of the report. You have to rerun it, and when you're done I want you to do Stacy's report and Alan's report for the next two weeks so you get it through your head how to run this correctly."

We all make mistakes. They often need to be corrected. That's life. It's how we learn. One of those responses from your supervisor is supportive and going to inspire you to do it again—correctly this time (and chances are you won't forget next time). The other is going to make you hop on Indeed and start looking for a new job.

On the other side, when the consequence lacks proportionality in the other direction, it becomes meaningless. If your boss bailed you out and had your coworker redo your report, or your dad basically cleaned up the mess for you, it likely wouldn't result in any change. While it's better to err on this side of things, you may need to be willing to allow your child to be a little *more* uncomfortable than is naturally comfortable to you.

Collaborative Discipline

There is one more dimension of good consequence imple-
mentation that I want to talk about, and it's probably the most
effective tip for logical consequence usage in kids over the
age of five. Determine your consequences *collaboratively.*

In collaborative discipline, you bring the child behind the
curtain and allow them to speak into the consequences and
restoration process directly. Ideally, they get to decide what
type of consequence or discipline will be most effective for
them. There are so many benefits of this style of discipline
that I could write an entire chapter or even a book about this,
alone.

When you engage kids in the discipline process collaboratively, they are always more invested in the process and usually
less likely to push back on the consequences or boundaries
they themselves helped set up.

They also build valuable life skills for how to set up systems
in adolescence and adulthood to regulate their *own* behavior.
Ultimately the goal of *all* discipline is to foster in your children
self-discipline: the ability for them to consider and control their
own actions and behaviors. The punishment-free parent
achieves this through modeling as well as conscious and
thoughtful interactions, building a lifelong relationship of trust
and security with their kids and eventually disciplining themselves out of a job.

Wise parents come to terms with the reality that they basically have twelve to fifteen years to discipline effectively
through conversation, consequences, modeling, and, as we'll
talk about in the next chapter, boundaries. If you do a *really*
good job of this, your child might opt to continue to come to
you for advice and support for the rest of your life . . . but at

that point, you're obviously an advisor, not an authority. If you reject all the foundations and mindsets I'm talking about in this book, you might have as few as ten years before your child effectively stops listening to you altogether and hides all of their problematic behavior. You'll have been deemed an irrational, unresponsive, punitive, and therefore *unhelpful* source of support.

The last benefit may come as a surprise, but it really shouldn't. By age six, your child very well may know themselves better than you know them. They have an entire inner world that we are just not privy to, and that means that, with support, they're going to be way better at coming up with an effective form of discipline than we are.

We often just go around assuming that our kids have no idea why they do things or how to stop. It might be true that they sometimes lack the awareness to know when they have an unmet need or lack the impulse control to stop themselves from acting out, but with our help, they can overcome many of those developmental deficiencies. It just takes getting curious rather than furious. It takes becoming emotional detectives, as we'll talk about in a couple chapters, and training them to do the same.

The end result of letting them drive is that, well, they learn how to drive. And isn't that the whole point in the first place?

Putting Collaborative Consequences into Practice

A few months ago my wife and I noticed that my seven-year-old was having trouble with his iPad. It manifested in numerous ways, but here are the highlights:

- When we set a boundary about what the iPad could be used for at certain times—for example, Minecraft Creative mode or educational games but *not* YouTube—he would struggle to not violate those terms.
- When it was time to get off the iPad, regardless of whether we gave him five-minute warnings or set timers, it was frequently a battle. Often, to hold the time boundary I would resort to actually physically taking the device away, an action I always try to avoid, and which is often met with aggression.
- He was using the device any chance he got, returning to the iPad whenever he had a spare minute. If we stopped actively engaging with him to care for a sibling or answer a phone call, he would disappear into a corner with the iPad, sometimes going as far as to hide with it. He was no longer coming up with creative or active ways to alleviate boredom, which is a necessary skill to develop in childhood.

My wife and I talked about it, and we decided we needed to intervene and problem-solve with him. The next day, it came time to get off the iPad. He refused, and I eventually had to take it. But I stopped him short before he went into full-on rage.

"Buddy! I want you to think about how you feel right now. You can be as mad at me as you want, but remember this feeling while you do. We'll talk about the iPad a little later."

A few hours later we talked about it, and I drew his attention back to how he felt in the moment when I took the iPad and held the boundary.

"I was so mad at you I wanted to punch you," he said.

Quick aside, no one gets in trouble for what they "wanted to do" in our house, so he offered that freely to me.

"Yeah, that's what I thought too! I could tell!" I replied, excited that he was able to be emotionally aware and reflect. I continued, "Do you think you would have had that feeling if you hadn't been playing iPad?"

"No. I only usually feel like that when I get hurt or I'm playing iPad."

Boom. Awareness. It was what I hoped for. What he was experiencing, I knew, was the dopamine letdown all of us (but especially those among us who have ADHD) get when we stop a particularly dopamine-inducing activity. What we know from research is that tablets are dopamine superchargers.[5] It can be almost *painful* for kids who are becoming addicted to their tablet to be torn away.

"Yeah! I think that's because our brains kinda freak out when we use the iPad too much and then have to stop all of a sudden. We go into rage mode."

"Yeah! Definitely!" he replied. It was clear he was tracking.

"Do you like feeling like that?" I asked.

"No."

"Yeah, I bet. I don't like it either. Sometimes I feel like that when you or your brothers interrupt me while I'm making WHOLE Parent videos on my phone. I really don't like it." I go on, "You know, I'm not just worried that you're getting that feeling when it's time to stop. It also seems like you're using the iPad every spare second you have. And also it sometimes feels like we say, 'Don't use YouTube,' but then you forget or your thinking brain seems to shut off, and five minutes later, you're back on YouTube."

"Yes! That definitely happens too," he replied.

"OK, I'm glad I'm not wrong and that you see it too. What do you think would help you to not feel this way and turn the iPad into a tool you use rather than a tool using you?"

"I don't know. Maybe give me five-minute warnings?"

"Yeah, I thought about that too, but we're already doing that most of the time and it doesn't seem to help. What else?"

"Maybe take a break?"

"Good idea! I also take breaks from my phone when it feels like I'm using it too much. How long do you think?"

"One day."

"Hmm, I'm not sure if that's long enough. I think we need a bigger reset. I want you to really get free of this tough cycle."

"A month?"

"Wow, that would be a long time," I said. "How about two weeks and then we can reassess? Should we put a date on the calendar so we can keep track?"

"Yes!"

"OK. I think this is a good starting point. Should I change the passcode on your iPad so it doesn't tempt you?"

"But, um, Dad? Can I still listen to audiobooks while I draw even though that's on the iPad?"

"Does listening to audiobooks while you draw make you feel the way we're talking about?"

"No, definitely not."

"Well then, I think it makes sense that we can start the audiobook and then you can still play and pause on the lock screen without using the passcode. If it gets turned off somehow, just come find me or Mom and we'll turn it back on."

"OK! Can I actually do that now? It sounds fun."

"Yup, which book?"

At this point my son literally handed me the iPad that had been sitting on the table so that I could change the passcode.

I'm not naive. Most of you are going to think I just made that story up. It *feels* unbelievable that a seven-year-old would do that. It would be even more unbelievable if you knew him. But when we combine all of the basic principles I'm talking about in this book, the results *are* unbelievable.

Often when parents feel like the discipline they're employing isn't working, they double down. Rather than question whether the discipline methods they're using are the right tool, they just assume that the discipline, usually punishment, wasn't severe enough to "take." I can't stress this enough. If your child continues to do the same problematic things over and over, it is not a sign of a moral failing, or that your child is a "bad kid," or that you need to try harder to control them through punishment. It is a clue that the way you're choosing to discipline them is not working and there is a better way.

5

Boundaries

Children learn how to make good decisions by making
decisions, not by following directions.

—ALFIE KOHN

"But they don't have to wear a helmet!" my son whined.
"Yes, I know that. Their parents don't have that rule,
but yours do. We always wear helmets when we ride bikes," I
said.

"But that's not fair! Wally is younger than me! If he doesn't
have to wear a helmet, why should I?"

"Well, when Wally rides *our* bikes he has to wear a helmet,
but I don't get to make choices about his family's rules."

"I'm not wearing one! You can't make me!" My son crossed
his arms, daring me to challenge him.

Taking a deep breath, I crouched down in an effort to not
further escalate the situation. "I understand that you're upset,"
I said. "I get it. It doesn't feel fair when I'm making you do
something your friends don't have to do. You can be as mad at
me as you want, but I cannot let you ride your bike without a
helmet."

"You can't stop me!" He grabbed the bike and tried to get on.

I moved to stand in front of the bike, holding both handlebars. At this point, the pre-punishment-free parent in me wants to scream in his face that "I'm in charge." That I can stop him if I want and will grab the bike I got him and take it away for a month. Instead, I take a deep breath, centering myself and reminding myself that it *does* feel unfair to him—that he's not giving me a hard time, he's having a hard time.

"I'm sorry, buddy," I said, "but I'm not going to let you ride unless you put on your helmet. I can go put the bike in the shed if it's too hard for you to follow this rule."

"*No!*" My son stormed away, throwing his helmet on the ground, and stomped into the house away from me, the bike, and his helmetless friends.

Boundaries, in many ways, are the counterpoint to consequences. When the natural consequences of a given behavior are too damaging or harmful to a child, it's up to us to set and hold a boundary.

Setting and holding boundaries is hard, but it's also one of your jobs. Just because you ditch punishment doesn't mean your kids are always going to *like* the things you say or do. When parents who grew up in punishment environments move into a punishment-free model of parenting, there is always the *potential* for overcorrection. This overcorrection most commonly manifests as parents who fail to embrace their role as boundary setters. When they do that, they fall into the trap of becoming "permissive parents."

Before we launch into all that, let's do a quick recap on why most misbehavior happens.

REASONS KIDS TEND TO MISBEHAVE	
Reasons Unrelated to Parenting	Reasons Related to Parenting
They're doing developmentally appropriate things that are socially inappropriate.	Problematic behavior is being modeled.
They are communicating everyday unmet needs.	The parents are routinely failing to meet basic needs.
They are testing or trying out new things to learn.	The parent lacks the ability or will to set boundaries.

It's this last item that we're going to focus on for the rest of this chapter.

If you've known any human children, you know they don't always make the best choices, but that doesn't mean we should make all their choices for them. In fact, the way that kids learn how to make choices is *by making choices*.

But just because we grant our children age-appropriate autonomy doesn't mean we totally abandon them. Keeping our children's bad choices from having lifelong consequences is still one of our primary jobs. After all, sometimes the natural consequences of their actions are just too great to allow.

The Problem of Permissiveness

Permissive parents are parents who really struggle to say "no" even when they need to. In the helmet example, a real conversation I had with my own son, I was preventing him from having the potential lifelong consequence of permanent irreversible brain damage. To me, the natural consequence of winding up with a potentially debilitating brain injury was too much.

Not every parent has that boundary (as my son was quick to point out). But not every parent has a spouse, brother, mother, and sister-in-law who have worked in and around the Emergency Department at the hospital for a cumulative century. Not every parent has a mother-in-law who spent the better part of her career treating people with traumatic brain injuries. And frankly, not every parent spends a wildly disproportionate amount of time thinking about kids' brains. But I do. So for me and my wife, it is a rule—a boundary that has been set. I'm not going to give in, even if every last one of the fifty-plus kids in our neighborhood rides around with wind blowing through their hair.

A parent who struggles with permissiveness cannot easily do what I did. They give in, usually to keep the peace or even to be *liked*. Conflict with their child or even seeing their child express unhappiness with their boundaries is too much for a permissive parent. It feels easier and safer to just give in.

But boundaries go beyond simply preventing your kids from having traumatic brain injuries and other too-severe natural consequences. Because of the way kids' brains work, boundaries are, ironically, how they can experience the most freedom and growth.

Let me explain using a hypothetical "perfect playground" as an example.

Here's how I define a perfect playground. The playground, first and foremost, has to be set back away from the street or at least fenced properly. Second, the playground should feature equipment designed for a specific age range of kids. Third, the playground must be well cared for, with no broken equipment and an extra-thick layer of mulch over the play space.

The reason this playground is perfect for me is because it represents a place where, depending on the ages of my kids, they can play totally *independently* from me. This playground, in other words, has proper *boundaries*. There is a boundary around the playground to prevent the kids from wandering off and being hit by a car. It has boundaries on the types of equipment available based on the ages it's designed for. And when inevitably a kid does fall off the slide—they'll have a *soft-enough* landing to prevent major harm. Because the architect designed the park with these boundaries, when I show up with my (appropriately aged) kids, I can let them be totally and completely free and autonomous.

That is the ideal in setting boundaries. Creating an environment for *reasonably safe freedom*. Good boundaries create an environment where kids can do as they please, learning and developing in a whole host of ways they do best *without* adult intervention, and without risking severe harm. Sure, kids can (and will) still fall off this perfect playground and get a bruise or a scrape, but these are appropriate and reasonable risks that may hurt a little in the moment but will, in the long run, help them learn, gain confidence, and be more resilient.

Going back to the helmet example, because my wife and I intentionally set that boundary and held it firm, my son, who has long since accepted that he has to abide by the boundary, now has more agency to play with his bike and go up and down the sidewalk as he pleases, often without supervision. He races his friends, puts skid lines in the driveway, and even dives off of his moving bike into the grass when the game calls for it.

If I failed to hold that boundary, knowing what I know about traumatic brain injuries, I would undoubtedly be far more controlling. Instead of a handful of rules—chief among them "wear your helmet"—I would have a never-ending list of dos and don'ts. This is ultimately the problem with failing to set appropriate boundaries for kids. You wind up having to assert *more* control and, in the end, you usually default back to your factory parenting settings. The more boundaryless the parental environment, the more direct control the parent has to leverage, and ultimately the more likely the parent is to resort to punishment. It's a trade-off most parents never think about.

The other thing is, kids thrive when they have freedom within boundaries. As confident and bold as they might seem on the outside, kids inherently know how vulnerable they are. They look to adults, especially their parents, to help them understand the world and survive in it. When their parents seem to have no boundaries, it places too much perceived responsibility on the child. While age-appropriate responsibility and autonomy promotes long-term positive outcomes, *boundaryless* parenting does the opposite.

A World Without Boundaries

I remember a friend from high school whose parents had effectively no boundaries—for themselves or for her. They were both immature and erratic caregivers who often were so emotionally dysregulated that they rarely seemed to care at all what she did. When they did care, usually all of a sudden, it was because of their own issues, not because they'd identified a safety risk for her or her siblings. While they put on a front of promoting independence, it could probably better be described as *indifference*.

As a result, she knew there were no safety nets for her. Even though she could do whatever she wanted, she actually went through the world with far less perceived freedom than most of our other peers who had reasonable boundaries. She was afraid to make mistakes because she never knew which mistakes would turn out to be catastrophic.

This is how boundaryless kids live. The world, so scary and unpredictable to their underdeveloped brains, becomes that much scarier and more unpredictable when their parents aren't seen as a trustworthy source of safety. Kids who grow up with boundaries know that ultimately, if their parents are permitting them to do something, that thing is probably at least reasonably safe.

My son, highly sensitive though he is and usually very nervous about getting hurt, can be seen flying by on his bike. Why? Because his parents have boundaries around that activity, and he understands that boundaries are fundamentally about keeping him safe. As long as he stays within those boundaries, he can have a reasonable assumption of safety. He doesn't have to rely on his underdeveloped brain's untrustworthy ability to determine the relative safety of a given activity. He can rely on us.

"Because I Said So"

When we set boundaries we also have to be honest, both with our kids and ourselves, about why a given boundary is a boundary. If we merely say "because I said so"—a common justification among the last generation of parents—we miss out on the opportunity to help our kids learn to set *their own* boundaries in the future. That's the thing about boundaries: Even though they change as kids grow up, people don't grow out of needing boundaries. We all need them, not just kids, and when we help kids understand why we have set a boundary in place, we actually set them up for long-term success.

It is also important to be honest with ourselves about why we set certain boundaries. Often, the boundaries that we set are not grounded in our own logical considerations about parenting but are instead just carried over from the boundaries, logical or not, that our parents set for us.

I'm thinking about something like profanity. In my house growing up, it was a boundary that we didn't swear, but there was no defined *reason* for the boundary, at least that I can remember. It was one of those "because I said so" kinds of rules. We could easily have been taught which words had potentially negative impact in certain social situations and have *also* had the space to use them in the safety of our family, but instead it was just a rule. It was only when my wife brought this to my attention when I overreacted to my oldest's first colorful words that I realized that it was a boundary I just didn't need to hold over. Instead, we had a conversation about what those words mean, how people use them, and why there are plenty of times and places where we should probably choose to use other words.

On the other hand, there are plenty of places where my parents didn't set boundaries that I am choosing to set for my kids: things like video games, screen usage, and social media. Some of that is a sign of the times. There was no social media when I was a preteen, and we know much more now about the potential harm to children from early or prolonged exposure to those things.[1] Even so, I was just lucky.

Many of my classmates and I would often play video games for basically the entire weekend without stopping. Some of them developed an almost addictive obsession with games like *Call of Duty,* and to this day they spend hours and hours in a fantasy world rather than getting a job or fostering positive in-person relationships.

Of course their parents—like my parents, who had their first kid before the original Nintendo was even released—had no way of knowing the potential consequences.

There's so much we don't know, so many ways we might accidentally fall into some difficult thing we didn't foresee. But as hard as it is for us to guess where the boundaries should be, it's much harder for our kids with a fraction of the life experience and complex reasoning. That's why it's important to set boundaries, and also assess whether those boundaries are good or helpful for keeping our kids safe on a regular basis.

Changing the Rules

However, you can and *should* change your boundaries sometimes.

Whether it's considering the effectiveness of a boundary or responding to the development of your child, most boundaries have to be adjusted over time. Getting back to our "perfect playground" analogy, boundaries, just like the playground equipment, change with age.

You might have a boundary that your three-year-old can't

play unsupervised in the front yard. It's a reasonable boundary for a three-year-old, as they usually don't remember how important it is to stay out of the street and are far more likely to just wander off. But if you have that same boundary for a six-year-old, well, it might be time to reconsider.

The developmental capacity of your kids dictates the boundaries. If you don't adjust, kids will quickly realize that the boundary is no longer there for their flourishing and safety and has become an arbitrary rule to be followed simply for the sake of obedience.

You don't want to end up in that place because the boundaries that *are* still in place for their safety will be disregarded too. When you demand obedience for obedience's sake, the problematic behavior usually doesn't stop; it just goes underground. And when problematic behavior goes underground, you lose all ability to curtail and speak into it.

I've seen this play out numerous times in working with parents and even teens. When a parent creates unreasonable boundaries that do not take into consideration the age and stage of their child, the boundaries become ineffective. The parent who tries to tell their teenager that they cannot date usually has the best intentions of trying to protect their child from becoming physically intimate beyond their emotional capacity or in ways that violate their personal values or religious convictions. The problem is, usually this takes the form of setting up boundaries that allow no relational and physical exploration . . . which almost always backfires. As a result, the teen just takes the relationship underground, where the parent has effectively no oversight. Often, the parent finds out and then tries to double down on the rules, leveraging a punishment to try to take back control. They restrict cell phone access, take away computer privileges, ground them, and even remove their bedroom door. The teen then sees how seemingly irrational the parent has become and, coupled with the humiliation that often follows, decides that *none* of the parent's rules or boundaries are valid, pushing them to engage in the relationship with total disregard for safety.

In *Romeo and Juliet,* the play someone probably tried to make you read but you just remember watching the Leonardo DiCaprio version in high school English, the conflict is centered on what happens when parents of teenagers set *unreasonably strict boundaries.* The teenagers sneak around anyway and often go to extreme lengths to be together, which results in some pretty extreme consequences (spoiler alert: they both end up dead).

On the other hand, the parents who have adjusted their boundaries to allow for the teen to feel like they have a sense of agency and autonomy usually gain the trust and respect of their child—leading, ultimately, to the most important boundaries still being maintained.

When parents do their best to say "yes" as much as possible, they make their "no" far more powerful.

I'm using an example of teenagers here, but the same thing applies to multiple developmental stages in children. If you refuse to adjust your boundaries to accommodate the growth and development of your child, they will cease to trust the boundaries.

So what do we do when we need to hold certain boundaries that are nonnegotiable but our kids don't like it? We communicate clearly and empathetically. Let's start with the "clear" part.

Communicating Clearly and Empathically

Do not euphemize or waffle around your boundaries. State them clearly and do not waver. This may feel unkind in the moment, but it's actually the kindest possible way to communicate boundaries. It's unkind to give kids false hope where they feel like they can get around a boundary and then, in the end, you slam the door in their face and resort, usually in desperation, to your old punishing ways when they rebel.

Take the helmet example again. If I had said, "I don't know, buddy. I really think, maybe, we should try to wear a helmet when we ride our bike," it would have been ultimately unkind to my son. He would have assumed, because the boundary was set in such an unclear way, that it was up for negotiation or debate.

He would have concluded that if he argued his point convincingly enough about his friends not wearing their helmets that I might yield and give in to letting him also not wear his helmet. That would have resulted in more hurt feelings as, added to the disappointment about having to wear a helmet, he would also believe that it was his fault because he failed to convince me. In reality, I was never going to give in and let him not wear a helmet and I needed to communicate that.

If a boundary is truly set in stone for you at a given developmental stage, be as clear and informative as you possibly can be about it.

"Buddy, I cannot let you ride your bike without a helmet because if you fall you could get a really bad bonk and wind up in the hospital or worse. If I let you do that, I would not be doing my job as your dad."

But *clear* is only half of the boundary-setting formula. The

other half is being able to communicate those boundaries empathetically. This just means communicating those boundaries in a way that takes into account your child's perspective
and allows space for them to have emotions based on that
perspective.

I know that my son does not and cannot understand the
serious injuries that he could get as a result of riding his bike
without a helmet. His brain is just not developed enough yet
to assess risk proportionally. That means, from his perspective, what I'm saying feels mean and unnecessarily controlling. That's why in the example at the beginning of the chapter,
I made it clear to him that he is allowed to *feel* about the
boundary however he'd like. He can even express that emotion to me in whatever way he chooses. What he simply cannot do, for his own good, is violate the boundary. The boundary
is not in place based on his feelings; the boundary is in place
to keep him physically safe.

The Need to Fail

That said, the boundaries we set, as well as the other parenting tactics we deploy, must allow kids to take a reasonable
amount of risk and even come to a reasonable amount of
harm.

I've alluded to this in the last two chapters, but it needs
more explanation. If you asked me what the single greatest
failure of the modern "gentle parenting" philosophy is, it's
right here. Because millennials were often raised in such a
way that we are terrified of failure and making mistakes, we
do everything in our power to keep our kids' lives free from

failure and mistakes. The thing is, making small mistakes is the way that we learn how to not make big mistakes. When well-meaning millennial parents save their own kids from their mistakes, they're setting them up for *far* greater failure down the road.

Consider Dr. Farmer's civilizations class back in the chapter on consequences. What if he had followed the format of some of my grad school courses—and likely many of *his* grad school courses—where the only assessments were midterms and finals? That learning experience for me would have looked like a C- at best in his course, and that's if I could have persuaded one of my classmates to cough up their notes from the first half of the semester to save my skin.

I see this play out all the time at the park. I normally don't take my kids to parks where, without my intervention, they have a risk of serious injury. That's the boundary setting in action.

Assuming I'm comfortable with the park's existing boundaries, I'll intentionally sit on a bench, or even a dozen feet behind the benches, deliberately not intervening with my kids as they play. Regularly, I'll see a dad or mom following a half step behind their own three-year-old toddler, hands twitching, ready to catch them if they start to show *any* signs of slipping on the first step of the playground stairs.

Half the time they're so caught up in the steady stream of "Be careful! Don't do that! You're not big enough for that! Do you need help? Here, I'll bring you down" that they won't even notice my two-year-old now four feet off the ground, confidently climbing up the rounded ladder on the other side of the playground; the very same one they just essentially carried their very able-bodied child up.

If they do notice him, they'll usually scream and sprint toward him like he's about to fall into a hundred-foot rock quarry. At that point, it's a race, and because it's happened enough times, I'm ready for it.

Choosing to not intervene is not the same as being inattentive.

I almost always get there first and stop the random well-meaning stranger from grabbing him or scaring him. What follows is often some sort of scolding where they give me, the "distracted dad," who they assume probably never watches his own kids, a lecture about how my son could have gotten *really* hurt.

If they seem like they're open to it, or I'm particularly snarky that day, I'll respond, "Really? Do you think he could have gotten *really* hurt? I feel like the worst that could happen is a broken bone. But as thick as the wood chips are here, probably not even that."

They will look at me absolutely flabbergasted. How dare I let a child play where there is *any* chance of injury?

Of course, they can't know that I picked this park specifically because of how it was designed. They can't know I don't bring my toddlers to places to play where there is a high chance that they'll get *really* hurt. They also can't know that my twenty-month-old has incredibly steady hands and is a gifted and focused climber precisely *because* he's been allowed to fall.

What they don't know, in other words, is that the reason I'm not worried about him climbing that four-foot ladder is that he's been allowed to fall and learn.

In writing this chapter I conducted an impromptu experiment where I sat for over an hour at a local playground designed for toddlers while my two- and three-year-old played.

The only times I intervened were when well-meaning adults would ask my three-year-old "Where is Mommy?" As I watched, over twenty different kids played on the equipment. Apart from a few older siblings, all the kids were between two and five years old. Not one single parent I saw was more than four feet away from their child at any point. These parents would often lunge for their kids when they showed any sign of unsteadiness. What were they so afraid of?

Obviously freak accidents happen, and I don't mean to belittle anyone who has had a child seriously injured or killed due to such an accident. Playground equipment isn't always well maintained and sometimes it fails. Freak accidents can happen . . . but we have to consider that it is exceedingly rare.

Our Conditioned Sensitivity to Risk

Because we live in the post-internet era, we are exposed to these "freak accident" stories so frequently that our brains disproportionately assess remote risks as greater than they really are. This is likely because our brains evolved to be overcautious and pay attention to things that could present a threat to our well-being or the well-being of our children.

For the better part of a century, news outlets have been learning to adjust and optimize news programs to keep us tuning in. It's just business. Tragic, depressing, horrifying headlines, especially concerning children, first sold papers, then drove Nielsen ratings, and now generate clicks.

The effect on our brains has been an increasingly unreasonable sensitivity to risk. In the same way our kids and teens often disproportionately *underestimate* the risks of actually dangerous things because they have an underdeveloped prefrontal cortex, we, in the post-internet era, have been conditioned to *overestimate* risks. Because we're exposed to exceedingly rare things so frequently, our brain cannot wrap itself around the reality that these things are, in fact, exceedingly rare.

Let me give you a couple of examples.

Out of the roughly 14 million American children who play baseball every year, three to four kids are killed in baseball-related injuries.[2] That means that the chance your child will die playing baseball is about .000025 percent. For reference, you are about 260 times more likely to be struck by lightning than your child is to die playing baseball. That said, I have a friend whose brother died at nine years old when he was hit in the head playing third base at the park. This makes him much more fearful than is reasonably proportionate when he thinks about his kids playing baseball.

Most people have a broad enough social circle to have one or two personal stories that bias them against an activity that has statistically minute risk. Before the information era those were the things parents would find themselves being unreasonably cautious about. The problem is, we don't live in a world anymore where we're only exposed to the terrible tragedies of the people we know. We are exposed to everyone's tragedies, all the time.

One of the most notable recent historical examples of this social macrophenomenon happened in the wake of the 9/11 World Trade Center attacks. Commercial flying has always been one of the safest ways to travel—far safer, in fact, than driving—and that didn't change after 9/11. Nevertheless, as a result of the hijackings the national demand for airline tickets plummeted by an unprecedented 30 percent, and over a decade later, the effects of the attacks were still negatively affecting demand.[3]

That's just what happens when we are exposed to traumatic and horrifying things, regardless of how statistically insignificant they are to our actual well-being. This shouldn't surprise us. Our survival brain takes over and makes us irrational even when the threat is merely perceived and not actually threatening.

But this becomes a unique problem in modern parenting.

Technically speaking, there has never been a safer time in human history to be a child in most of the world. With vaccines, research, and modern medicine absolutely decimating child and infant mortality, more children are living to see adulthood than ever before. I've asked dozens of parents whether they feel like child abductions are more or less common now than when they were kids, and I have yet to meet one person who has said "less common." But that perception is not grounded in reality. In fact, the likelihood of a child being stereotypically kidnapped[4] is as low as it has ever been. Better news still is that, according to experts like David Finkelhor, who studies child kidnappings, kidnapped children today have the lowest likelihood of dying as a result of the kidnapping than at any time on record.[5] In fact, according to Warwick Cairns in his book *How to Live Dangerously,* your child has approximately a .0002 percent chance of being kidnapped by a stranger. "Or, to put it another way, it would take your child, left outside, 500,000 years to be abducted by a stranger. . . ."[6]

When we set our boundaries, we need to set them with this knowledge and reasoning in mind and not just based on our emotions or perception. Regardless of how we may feel and what our amygdala seems to be telling us, it's never been safer to be a child—at least out in the real world.

Too Many Boundaries?

On the other hand, there is a looming threat to all of our kids—a threat that, as much as anything else, initially launched me into this work of understanding child development.

That threat is the growing mental health crisis among teens and children.

According to the Centers for Disease Control and Prevention, between 2010 and 2019 feelings of persistent hopelessness and sadness—as well as suicidal ideation and behaviors—increased by about 40 percent among young people.[7] This was all *before* the pandemic, which most experts believe dramatically exacerbated the problem. Other sources identify that the "post-pandemic" (2021) rates of suicide among people ages ten to twenty-four increased by 62 percent.[8]

Make no mistake, everything in this book is, at least in part, about combating this increase. As I wrote every chapter, I had this reality in the back of my mind. But for our purposes now I want to talk about one factor in fostering resilience that we haven't yet touched: autonomy.

According to Jonathan Haidt in his 2024 book *The Anxious Generation: How the Great Rewiring of Childhood Is Causing an Epidemic of Mental Illness,* the two key factors driving the adolescent mental health crisis today are children's unfettered access to technology and the internet (especially social media) and the increasing trend for parents to fail to give their children healthy autonomy in the real world.[9] In other words, parents' failure to set boundaries around technology use (specifically giving kids their own smartphones before high school and social media access before sixteen years old), plus parents' overprotective boundaries around real world autonomy, are two main drivers of this devastating trend.[10]

I've been letting my younger kids fall off playground equipment for as long as they've been able to crawl, in no small part because the research supports the conclusion that letting your kids have agency and autonomy—including to make mistakes and suffer from the minor consequences of those mistakes—helps to build the resilience that they need to thrive. The more control a parent attempts to assert over their children through what we might call overprotective boundary setting (aka helicopter parenting), the less likely the child is to be able to cope with and regulate overwhelming emotions.[11]

On the contrary, children who are granted age-appropriate autonomy tend to have better emotional outcomes. I believe it's because of what autonomy communicates to children. Autonomy says, "You got this. I trust you." And then when kids fall or fail, loving and attentive parents are there to pick them up, dust them off, and help them learn. As a result, kids learn to place their failures and mistakes in context. Not only do they tend to make that mistake less often in the future, but they also learn that they can and will overcome difficult things.

When we've developed neural pathways around correcting and contextualizing mistakes and failure, we can rely on those neural pathways when the next unforeseen challenge arises. This gives our kids grit and resilience both in adolescence and throughout their adult lives.

This is why balance is so critical in boundary setting. Not enough boundaries—especially, it seems, around technology usage—and your child will be lost in the void of not knowing what is safe and what is not. Too many boundaries, or an inability or unwillingness to adjust boundaries, can contribute to anxiety and depression on the other side.

I imagine it feels, after reading that last sentence, like parents are somehow expected to thread an impossible needle, but it's really not as difficult as it sounds. It just requires shifting your mindset a bit. Becoming an overbearing helicopter parent who prevents failure, mistakes, and setbacks at all costs should not be the goal. Instead, you can be a stable source of love and support in the midst of life's bumps and bruises, failures and disappointments. In other words, instead of trying to be the parent who catches your kids when they fall off the playground, be the parent who picks them up off the ground when they do.

6

Unleashing Our Emotional Superpowers

> Emotion regulation starts with giving
> ourselves and others the permission to
> own our feelings—all of them.
>
> —MARC BRACKETT

When I was a little kid, I lived two doors down from my best friend in the whole world, Billy. Billy's dad was a part-time tow truck driver, part-time semiprofessional race car driver. Their garage, on the alley that we grew up playing in, was filled with every shiny chrome tool imaginable and smelled of old oil, gasoline, and cigarette smoke. There always seemed to be half a car in there with at least one grown-up, covered in black grime and dirty oil, lying on their back underneath it.

My dad had a cool job too, to be sure. He donned business clothes and grabbed his briefcase on the way out the door to work for a company called Champro, which made sports equipment. It was no Nike, with its flash and cultural prestige, but I always had a new quality baseball glove or basketball whenever I wore out the old one. It was a privilege that I only now fully appreciate.

Even so, as all kids do, I spent many days envious of my

friend Billy. His dad was basically always around and using cool (and obnoxiously loud) tools. My envy reached its height when one day Billy's dad did the same thing for him that my dad had been doing for me for my entire life. He leveraged his job to get Billy something fun.

It was a go-kart. My guess is Billy's dad had found it somewhere or bought it off the junkyard he sold parts to. One day, instead of taking apart a dilapidated junk car or tuning up the engine on his race car, Billy and I found his dad, Billy Sr., rebuilding and repurposing old parts he had lying around to make this go-kart live again . . . and in its resurrection, *way* too powerful for a couple of not-even-seven-year-olds.

When the engine turned over and Billy got behind the wheel, the green-eyed monster of jealousy in my six-year-old chest roared. Billy, always the rebel, put his foot to the floor and shot off down this alley full of cars pulling out of blind corners at death-defying speeds. When he had sufficiently had his "turn," the kart pulled to a stop in front of me, and in an act of parenting that is quintessential '90s, Billy Sr. offered me a chance to drive without even considering whether to first consult my parents.

I am happy to report I was more cautious and stayed in the empty parking lot next to Billy's house, not daring to venture out into the center of the alley that my parents had instilled a healthy fear of. By some massive stroke of luck, neither I nor Billy wound up visiting my mom at work in the emergency room that day.

That night, over dinner, I told to my parents about the exhilarating experience of first-grade go-kart driving. Judging by the speed of the kart Billy now had, I was fairly sure I could make it to school as fast or faster than taking the bus once my parents got me one too. It seemed like a win-win. My parents could spend a little on a similar kart and I would save them the hassle of dropping me off or picking me up from school.

They wanted to see the kart for themselves. I realize now as a parent myself to a child who has survived past the age of six, they wanted to see it firsthand not because there was a snowball's chance in hell that I was getting one, but to determine whether I would ever be allowed at Billy's house again. So when we heard the telltale sound of the kart roaring up and down the alley, we all went out to see it.

I never looked up at my parents' faces, likely grimacing in horror as they saw this tiny, blond-haired, blue-eyed child—who looked uncannily like one of their own children, with no safety gear to speak of—ripping up and down the alley at ridiculous speeds. I had eyes only for the kart: the object of my envy.

Whether my dad had a conversation with Billy Sr. about never letting me near that death trap, I never asked. What I remember is going back inside and hearing that my *feelings* about the go-kart were wrong. Envy and jealousy are bad feelings we need to prevent and avoid. I remember coming to the unmistakable conclusion that I *shouldn't* feel that way.

This conclusion was reinforced dozens of times over the next decade. When I went to church, I heard about how coveting, the fancy church word for "jealousy," wasn't just a bad feeling to have, it was a *sin*—and a bad one at that, making the list of "Top 10" sins along with murder, perjury, adultery, and being disrespectful to your parents. From then on, whenever I felt jealous, whether over my friends getting the next-gen video game system or over those super-cool Cartoon Network commercials for Batman action figures, I always stopped short of telling my parents. Jealous was a bad way to feel, and if you felt it, *you were bad*. And I didn't want anyone, especially my parents, to think I was bad.

Early Conditioning and Emotional Intelligence

In 1995, science journalist and doctor of psychology Daniel Goleman published *Emotional Intelligence: Why It Can Matter More Than IQ*. Almost overnight it became an international bestseller, introducing the concept of emotional intelligence (EQ) to the general public. The book resonated across educational and corporate sectors, leading to the development of emotional literacy programs and corporate training alike. Smack-dab in the middle of the decade that the neuroscience community has since coined "the decade of the brain," everyone started caring about emotional intelligence.

Why is this important? Because the overwhelming majority of us, the parents of today, were born before 1995. More than that, virtually all of our parents were well into adulthood before 1995. Simply put, as important as emotional intelligence might be to you today, what we know about emotional intelligence today had virtually zero impact on our parents' most formative years.

Today, whether you're in the field of education, sales, human resources, marketing, ministry, healthcare, or management, the importance of emotional intelligence is likely to be impressed upon you by one training or seminar or another. Why? Because thirty years later we now know for certain that Goleman was right.

The most successful and impactful thinkers, leaders, and creative minds in the world are not those with the highest IQs but the ones with the most emotional intelligence.

While cognitive abilities are certainly important for success in business and interpersonal relationships, it is emotional intelligence that is far more predictive of long-term success and fulfillment. And unlike IQ, according to Goleman, EQ can be learned:

> Emotional intelligence can be learned and this is the good news. Unlike IQ which doesn't change from birth, it's really an index of how quickly the brain can learn, every emotional intelligence skill is learned and learnable. Children start to learn it, you know, when you're an infant and your mom or your dad picks you up when you're crying and helps you calm down, that's a lesson in emotional intelligence. We learn it through life.[1]

In this way, our children's ability to be emotionally intelligent and act based on that intelligence is one of the most important skills they will ever learn. More than algebra, sentence structure, or the scientific method, it is what they know about emotions that will change their life for the better. But far too often emotional intelligence is not measured or taught in any systematic way, in schools or at home.

It's not just the kids. Many adults lack the robust emotional intelligence commensurate with their age and stage of development. Try this exercise. Set a timer for sixty seconds. Sit down with a piece of paper or the notes app on your phone and just list all of the emotions that you can think of. It might help to think back over the last week and consider which emotions you remember experiencing during that time. At the end of the minute, when the timer goes off, look at your list. How many emotions are there? Ten? More than ten?

If the answer is more than three, according to Brené Brown's research presented in *Atlas of the Heart,* you're above average in emotional intelligence.² That's right; the average adult can name only "happy, sad, and angry." That represents, by my calculation, about one percent of the words for emotions that are available to us English speakers. The crisis of Emotional *Ignorance* is a social epidemic.

The thing is, we have known for a long time and have now proved through neuroimaging that a person's ability to label and adequately name the emotions they are experiencing is a key component to the processing and regulation of those emotions. What this means is that if most adults can only think of three emotions off the top of their head, chances are, they are only aware and able to adequately process a *fraction* of the emotions they are experiencing.

If we continue to allow ourselves to be emotionally ignorant and pass that on to our children, we are placing them at a severe disadvantage, not only for their long-term success in relationships and career, but also in their ability to become mentally and emotionally healthy adults.

Embracing Feelings

So is the cure just memorizing a giant list of emotion words and drilling them into our kids with flash cards? No. Because for most of us this is not a vocabulary issue. If I listed more complex emotions like "jealousy" or "excitement," you would know how to apply those and use them in a sentence. When someone tells you that they overheard a coworker say something profoundly ignorant and disrespectful and as a result they were "disgusted," you know exactly what they mean.

The problem isn't that we don't *know* enough feelings; the problem for most of us is we were conditioned to believe that many of the feelings we experience are to be kept inside our bodies, away from others—just like me with Billy and his new go-kart.

I want you to take a moment and think back on your childhood. This isn't meant to be an exercise in judging your parents; I certainly don't judge mine. Which feelings in your house were welcome and which were not?

If you were like me and most of the parents I work with, you were raised to prioritize some feelings and avoid or even suppress others. I call this process "learning to put emotions into buckets." Every family has emotions that kids are encouraged to express publicly (within reason) and privately.

The thinking goes, "Children should always be happy. After all, we adults keep them fed, clothed, and housed. They get to go to school and play outside with their friends and they don't have to go to work or worry about bills. They live a comparably carefree life to us grown-ups. What do they possibly have to be sad, mad, or jealous about?"

The other reality is that for many of us, our emotions, at least at times, were too much for our parents to handle.

As I mentioned before, our parents, most of them Baby Boomers or very early Gen Xers, were already adults by 1995 when emotional intelligence became part of the cultural conversation. They were raised in a postwar era by people who were themselves survivors of the Great Depression and one or two world wars. Suppressing emotions was not only normal, it was expected, and your parents were likely taught to suppress their own "bad" emotions to a much greater extent than you were.

A lot of parenting methods in those days were designed to condition kids to be totally nonemotional. This was achieved by recommending that parents show their child essentially no affection and ignore or punish any "bad" emotion the child expressed. Emotions, and by extension emotional intelligence, were not only undervalued, but they were seen as the *enemy* of the modern, logical adult. In fact, many publications distributed by the U.S. government in the decades before our parents were born recommended to condition babies to be essentially nonemotional from birth. The "Bad Habits" section of one popular booklet, *Infant Care* from the Care of Children series, suggests that if "no cause for the crying can be found" (other than the child being scared or desiring connection) and mothers respond by comforting their children anyway, the child will become a "spoiled, fussy baby, and a household tyrant." The remedy, the booklet goes on, is to ignore the child, allowing them to cry alone in a dark room until they are conditioned to stop seeking connection. "This may sound cruel, and it is very hard for a young mother to do," *Infant Care* acknowledges, "but it will usually take only a few nights of this discipline to accomplish the result."[3]

One of the most influential proponents of these parenting methods was former president of the American Psychological Association John B. Watson, widely considered to be the founder of behaviorism. Back in the early twentieth century, he was lauded for his promotion of and personal adherence to raising *little adults*. In the Watsonian approach to parenting, as seen in the above booklet reference, parents were advised against providing too much—or in fact any—affection to their children. The thinking was, children should be treated as though they were tiny adults, with total disregard for their emotional intelligence level, brain development, coping skills, or physical developmental capacities. He famously said in his bestselling book on parenting:

> Never hug and kiss [your children], never let them sit on your lap. If you must, kiss them once on the forehead when they say goodnight. Shake hands with them in the morning. Try it out. In a week's time you will find how easy it is to be perfectly objective with your child and at the same time kind. You will be utterly ashamed of the mawkish, sentimental way you have been handling it.[4]

He believed, as is evidenced in the frankly shocking quote above, that affection would spoil children and hinder their development, something he had absolutely no basis for in retrospect. In fact, we now know that the opposite is true. But his theories nevertheless impacted generations of children.

It's notable to point out that of Watson's four children, three attempted suicide, one successfully. James, one of Watson's surviving children, says this about his childhood with his brother Bill, who tragically killed himself at age thirty-three:

> I honestly believe the principles for which Dad stood as a behaviorist eroded both Bill's and my ability to deal effectively with human emotion . . . and it tended to undermine self-esteem in later life, ultimately contributing to Bill's death and to my own crisis. Tragically, that's the antithesis of what Dad expected from practicing these philosophies.[5]

Watson's own children struggled throughout their lives with psychological symptoms and behaviors consistent with insecure and disorganized attachment and neglect, including depression and alcoholism, in spite of being raised in a relatively stable home with two parents and plenty of income.

A woman whom I counsel, now a grandmother, reflects on being raised this way herself, although less extremely. Difficult emotions were simply not allowed at home growing up in the fifties and sixties. You put on a face and you didn't let anyone know what was really going on. Her parents, she says now, were competent providers, but they showed her essentially zero physical affection throughout her childhood.

Make no mistake, Watson wasn't the only parenting expert out there. Psychologist Harry Harlow, a colleague of Abraham Maslow, conducted a now famous study with Rhesus monkeys in the 1940s to prove that love and affection were essential to development in children. John Bowlby and Mary Ainsworth, the pioneers of attachment theory, were simultaneously developing methods of observing human children to prove the same.

Then, in 1949, Dr. Benjamin Spock took the parenting scene by storm with what might be called a precursor to today's modern "gentle parenting" movement. While he was massively successful and popular among some audiences, the tides of culture shifted slowly. His approach to more attentive and nurturing parenting stood alone against the army of parenting "experts," including those who had been effectively endorsed by the government. These "experts" advocated for everything from spanking infants who were crying so hard they were having convulsions or cyanotic breath-holding spells (turning blue) to not having essentially any interaction with babies in order to *"not spoil them."*[6] In fact, in the half century following his bestselling book, opposition to Spock's most basic principles remained a hallmark of many staunchly authoritarian parents, especially those affiliated with religious fundamentalism.[7]

Is it a surprise that so many of our parents, raised when this type of parenting was the cultural context, struggled to emotionally regulate themselves? Should we be surprised that many of them became overwhelmed by our underdeveloped nervous systems when we lashed out emotionally? Why should we be surprised that the prevailing wisdom into the early 2000s was to ignore children who experienced the less ideal or more difficult feelings of life and responded with a tantrum? Or that one of the most notable parts of my own "new parent education" in 2016 was to have the labor and delivery nurses impress upon me and my wife that *you won't spoil your child by holding them too much*"?

And in spite of this, as recently as 2021, I had a colleague echo the advice of the "no parental affection era," when he told me his four-month-old was crying *because over the holidays she was held too much and got spoiled.*"

It was much easier for our parents to punish, reject, shame, and ignore the feelings that were too overwhelming for them than to attempt to co-regulate with us. It was never modeled to them and so they didn't know what to do. Thankfully, with years of difficult work and important research, we have come to know better.

The resulting mindset for most of the millennials who were raised this way and whom I now work with is the "buckets of good and bad feelings": one bucket of feelings to keep and experience, one to discard, ignore, and be ashamed of.

So what was in these buckets? Well, I bet you could make your own list based on your personal experience and childhood, and it might be helpful for you to do so, but here's my generalized list from working with many parents of our generation.

Some emotions in the "Good" bucket might be . . .

- Happiness
- Joy
- Love
- Gratitude
- Serenity
- Hope
- Inspiration
- Amusement
- Pride
- Admiration
- Satisfaction
- Peace

We were allowed to name these emotions. We were allowed to express them with our faces or with our words without caution (for the most part). These are the emotions our parents used to describe the future they hoped for us. Had you asked your parents what goals they had for their kids in 1990, there is a high likelihood that it would have sounded something like, "I want my children to be successful, happy, and healthy."

It's a nice sentiment to be sure, but, when you think about it, there is a lot of underlying pressure to be happy *regardless* of circumstances—pressure that many kids develop people-pleasing tendencies to satisfy.

On the other side of the coin are the emotions that were not celebrated. These are the emotions that you and I were probably shamed for or even *punished* for expressing. Depending on your religious upbringing, even feeling one of these, regardless of the expression, might be classified as a moral failing. These are the "Bad" bucket emotions, and they are to be avoided—and if impossible to avoid, repented of, hidden away, and certainly not expressed to anyone. Ever.

Some emotions in the "Bad" bucket might be . . .

- Anger
- Fear
- Jealousy
- Disappointment
- Disgust
- Guilt
- Despair
- Envy
- Contempt
- And sometimes sadness

You may be thinking back now and realizing that you don't remember expressing one or even most of these emotions in your childhood. Sure, you can likely point to a few times when you got really mad or scared (anger is one of the three emotions most adults can name), but beyond that you might have trouble pinpointing a time you felt, for example, jealous. One reason you might have trouble remembering is because when you felt jealous (like I did with Billy's go-kart) and expressed that to your parents, you were shamed or dismissed. That dismissal led to our rejection of that emotion and often the loss of the resulting memory.

As kids, we look to our parents to help us ground our existence and understand our reality, and so when our parents ignored, punished, or shamed us, our brains decided that this emotion was better left alone, suppressed and hidden, rather than experienced and remembered.

Never forget, children have an innate survival interest in their parents' generally liking them and being happy they are around, alive, and well. When children are hurt emotionally, physically, or socially for something as out of their control as having the wrong feeling, they can build all sorts of psychological walls and techniques to protect themselves. When these feelings were either rejected outright or more generally invalidated, finding nowhere to go and nothing positive to link to in the brain, the experience of the feeling became *implicit* rather than explicit.

The one "bad" emotion that doesn't quite fit with the rest of these where men are concerned is anger. In Western society we tend to make special allowances for anger if for no other reason than it is unavoidable. It's just so primitive we can't always suppress it. We would never consider anger an emotion to be actively sought and expressed, but the occasional outpouring of anger is *understandable*. This "special treatment" for anger winds up really confusing things. Many men equate dozens of difficult or challenging emotions with anger and then *express* them as anger. Whereas sadness, fear, disappointment, and guilt are taboo in "traditional" masculinity, anger is somewhat permitted.

This is why, when I see one of my kids fall headfirst down the stairs or close their hand in the automatic van door (both happened this week . . . to the same kid), I'm just as likely to get mad as anything else. Even though I talk about this stuff with parents every single day, all I felt in those moments was mad.

Upon reflection I realized in both cases I probably ought to have felt scared that he might have been severely hurt, sad that he was upset and in pain, and guilty that I wasn't in a position to protect him. But in the moment, I was just mad. Somewhere in my default settings, I internalized that anger is the only challenging emotion that was okay to feel. That's why, even today, big feelings for me often default to being expressed as anger.

No Bad Feelings

Here's the profound truth: There are no bad feelings. Feelings are, at their core, no different from anything else our body experiences. Just like thirst is the sensation we have when our body needs water, anger is the sensation we have when our body sees injustice, and romantic jealousy is the sensation we have when our body values our partner and desires to maintain exclusivity. Even though we don't judge ourselves for being thirsty, we often judge ourselves for other things our body experiences . . . and that judgment comes at a cost.

When we avoid uncomfortable feelings and teach our children to do the same, those feelings do not remain benign. Feelings that are hidden away, left unprocessed, and generally shoved down will fester and infect our general well-being and mental health. Feelings that we do not work through become feelings that work through us. Jealousy, despair, anxiety, overwhelm, boredom, fear, and guilt are not emotions to be avoided at all costs or feelings to be suppressed or discarded. That they should be avoided is a lie we must reject.

So what's the alternative?

We have to re-train ourselves and our kids to become *emotions detectives* instead of *emotions judges*.

Emotions detectives—what Dr. Marc Brackett, founder of the Yale Center for Emotional Intelligence, calls *emotion scientists*—are people who are *nonjudgmental* about their emotions, choosing to view their emotions as insights to be considered. Emotions judges, on the other hand, are those who view emotions in the way I've been describing: judging and often condemning themselves for emotions that are "bad."[8]

Just as physical sensations like thirst communicate to the brain that you need to drink some water, *feelings* are internal sensations that communicate other messages to your conscious mind. In this way, feelings are one of the primary ways our brain communicates with *itself*. Specifically, feelings are the way that our limbic brain, the part where the amygdala lives and which often notices many things our prefrontal cortex misses, communicates with our *conscious mind*.

If we were limited to experiencing the world around us only through our prefrontal cortex—the logical, rational part of the brain—we would miss a whole lot. To process the massive amount of sensory data we're constantly being exposed to, the prefrontal cortex must constantly screen out things it deems unimportant. That means, if you tried to make your decisions *only* based on your prefrontal cortex, there would be massive amounts of important data you would be missing at essentially every moment of your life. Imagine trying to decide whether you should marry a romantic partner or move in with them void of feelings. It sounds crazy until you consider that thousands of people every day try to do just that when they suppress their "bad" feelings of curiosity for the same gender . . . or the "bad" feelings of uneasy discontentment that's hinting that they or their partner are not fully bought-in on the relationship long-term.

When we accept and consider emotions as *detectives* we can make healthier, better decisions as a result. In short, when we choose to embrace our emotions without passing judgment and instead seek to understand the messages they convey, we unlock a profound *superpower* within ourselves.

This newfound ability allows us to navigate life's challenges with greater wisdom and resilience. And best of all, by modeling this emotional intelligence to our children, we empower them to live authentically and fearlessly, embracing the diverse spectrum of their emotional experiences. They learn to appreciate the richness of their feelings, no longer constrained by the limiting boundaries of internal emotional restrictions. In turn, they can forge more genuine connections with others, make more-informed decisions, and savor life's intricate nuances, fostering a profound sense of emotional well-being and personal growth.

Isn't that the future you *actually* want for your child? Not just to be arbitrarily "happy" in some vague sense but to truly live into all the unique nuanced facets of life? Don't you want their joys to be unrestricted by the internal emotions bucket system?

I know that feelings, especially the dark ones, probably feel at least a little scary to you, but so did that roller-coaster before you mustered up the courage to strap in and ride it. And you have to admit, the roller-coaster wouldn't have been nearly as fun without a little fear mixed in.

Despite how scary it might seem, until we deconstruct the "feelings bucket system" that was programmed into us because of conclusions drawn from now debunked mid-century "anti-emotions" parenting, we will never be able to live up to our potential as parents . . . and are doomed to repeat the cycle with our own kids. Learning to live with "no bad feelings" and teaching your kids to do the same can truly transform both of your lives.

7

Becoming Conscious

Between stimulus and response there is a space. In that space is our power to choose our response. In our response lies our growth and our freedom.

—VIKTOR FRANKL

This quote comes from philosopher and Holocaust survivor Viktor Frankl in his book *Man's Search for Meaning.* One of his prevailing ideas throughout the book is that a distinctive quality of humans is our ability to *not* follow a consistent stimulus with a conditioned response. Unlike other species that impulsively react, our brains possess the unique ability to pause and reflect, consider our actions and their consequences, and choose how to proceed. That said, we, like all animals, have neural pathways that make *not reacting* feel almost impossible in the moment. But it is possible, and the more we do it, the easier it gets. According to Frankl, the greater our progress in our ability to *respond* rather than react, the more growth and agency we will inevitably enjoy. This is because in this unique ability lies the key to both our freedom and the opportunity to live into our fullest potential as individuals and a species.

The fact that Frankl, a direct victim of one of the most unspeakable human atrocities in history, who spent more than three years in concentration camps, is the one offering this to us should be inspiring. If he, in spite of his unimaginably horrific circumstances, was able to overcome his propensity to react rather than respond, then all of us have hope for growth and eventually success in that area.

We as parents all possess, to varying degrees, the ability to choose to pause in the moment when our kids trigger us and respond rather than react. It's what I did, to my astonishment, on the deck with the red Sharpie with my then five-year-old.

As we learn from Frankl and modern psychology, our capacity to consistently choose to respond rather than react in the moment is reliant on several factors. One of them is our brain's innate ability to physically change over time. This trait called *neural plasticity* refers to the adaptive quality of our brain to adjust and rewire over time. Simply put, you are not stuck with the factory default settings and neural pathways you currently have, as I alluded to in the chapter on mirroring when we discussed "Blazing a New Trail." When you intentionally choose a new path rather than unconsciously reacting, you slowly build new neural pathways that become the new default. Like a muscle, the more we train ourselves through repetition to pause and respond, the greater our capacity and ability become to respond rather than react *regardless of circumstance*. This process of changing our default reactions necessarily requires both introspective awareness and understanding of our own triggers.

Not Blank Slates

There is a profound truth we must grapple with. Those paradigms from our upbringing, especially around punishment, compliance, respect, and our relationship to feelings, don't just dissipate; they're intricately woven into the fabric of our identities and worldviews. They persist within the deepest parts of our unconscious minds, quietly influencing our reactions, *especially* in our role as parents. In other words, none of us enters parenthood choosing in a vacuum how we will raise our children.

We cannot simply *will away* our default reactions, especially if we're unwilling to be honest with ourselves about our own childhoods and the triggers they've given us. None of us is a blank slate when we become parents. If we want to respond rather than react, then we must begin by unpacking our pasts.

This process of becoming aware of our inherited paradigms, childhood baggage, and triggers gets to the heart of what has been coined "Conscious Parenting" by Dr. Shefali Tsabary, and it's the focus of this chapter.

Inherited Paradigms and Unconscious Reactions

When our children echo the behaviors we were once reprimanded for, we don't just experience a fleeting moment of nostalgia or discomfort. Often it's a visceral, deep-seated "trigger," catapulting us back to those childhood moments where we stood vulnerable, misunderstood, and often afraid.

In those moments, your child essentially becomes a mirror, reflecting your buried traumas and unresolved emotions rather than radiating their own innocence.

It's important to distinguish here that the word "trauma" means different things to different people. For the purposes of this book, I'm using the word "trauma" more broadly to refer to those events that are experienced as particularly distressing in childhood, and I'm using the term "extreme trauma" to refer to events that commonly result in PTSD. Some may feel that it is belittling to those who have experienced the horrifying realities of war, assault, or profound loss to call commonly accepted parenting practices *traumatic*. I am sensitive to this view, but I still choose to use the word "trauma" because, as Dr. Gabor Maté, psychiatrist, parenting expert, and Holocaust survivor, so eloquently points out, "Trauma is not what happens to you. Trauma is what happens inside of you as a result of what happens to you."[1] This being the case, we must accept that for vulnerable children many things can be traumatic that seem otherwise to be totally benign because of the way the memory is internalized and stored.

It's no surprise, then, that in those moments of heightened emotions, parents often find themselves uttering the very words that were once hurled at them by their parents. These often are the phrases that we promised ourselves we'd never use. Yet here they are, escaping our lips, as if we've been transported back in time into our parents' oak cabinet kitchen.

It's crucial to recognize this dynamic, to become *conscious*, not in order to berate, punish, or shame ourselves, but to build awareness.

Before we go any farther into the book, it's important to point out that punishing yourself is no more effective than punishing your kids; neither brings positive results. This is something I had to learn as an adult through many hours of therapy.

At its best, this consciousness reminds us that while our children might evoke memories of our past, they are their own unique individuals.

They're not us.

They're not reliving our histories, our challenges, or our traumas. It's our responsibility to ensure that our unresolved emotions don't cloud our judgment or dictate how we parent them.

Where You End and Your Child Begins

Becoming more conscious parents requires learning personal differentiation. Personal differentiation is the place where you end and someone else begins. This can be tricky for parents, especially because there was a time when a literal cord meant that there *was* no place where you ended and your mother began.

But even after birth, the ways we care for our tiny humans are just so incredibly intimate and can make personal differentiation a bit fuzzy even after the cord is cut. We wash them and feed them and cuddle them and even change their diapers. They are totally and completely dependent on us.

And then they don't grow up all at once. It happens slowly. Combine that with the fact that we all have hormones that literally bond us to our offspring, and, yeah, personal differentiation? What is that?

Yet learning to embody this differentiation is massively important. Think about it. Is there anyone who can trigger you quite like your kids? Probably not. The reason is because sometimes we all get a little fuzzy on the *line* between parents and children.

I've seen perfectly calm, soft-spoken people yell themselves hoarse at their kids. I've seen CEOs who sit in hostile million-dollar negotiations totally melt down over not being able to reason with their toddler. I've seen doctors, cool as cucumbers in life-or-death situations, admit to me that they totally fall apart when it comes to their teenagers. It's me too. I am often incredibly empathetic, patient, and gracious to total strangers, but I struggle every single day to be that for my kids (whom I love infinitely more than the strangers).

The reason our kids specifically trigger us is that, in our difficulty with differentiation, they can become a mirror into our own past. When we fail to foster proper distinctions between ourselves and our kids, we often wind up triggered precisely because the thing they're doing hits us in *our own* childhood wounds.

They don't remind us in the sense that we consciously remember or reflect on a part of our childhood. They just trigger our nervous system to reactivate as if we were back in our childhood home in 1994 being scolded, shamed, or punished for the very thing they are doing in 2025. As my friend Dan Nicholas, a career psychologist, has told me numerous times, "There is no time in the mind." When our childhood wounds are triggered, we're thrust back into survival mode, this time with all the power, and we often react the same way our parents did.

In fact, once you become consciously aware of this, you may realize you even use the same problematic *phrases* your parents used with you.

To understand why this is, we have to talk a little bit about memory. In the first chapter, we talked about the fact that our children's learning centers go "offline" when they go into survival mode. When this happens, the amygdala, located in their limbic system (the emotions part of their brain), takes over and starts running the ship. What I didn't mention is that the limbic system, while not typically associated with what we call the "logical" part of the brain (the prefrontal cortex), is heavily involved in the making and storing of *memory*.

Memory 101

The process of making and storing memories is a collaborative venture between the limbic system and the prefrontal cortex. In the simplest terms, when we take in the sensory information, thoughts, and feelings associated with an event, our hippocampus (another part of the limbic system) stores it and eventually organizes it into something the brain can draw on later.[2]

Think of this process as the assembly of a puzzle. The information our brain takes in is like a bunch of puzzle pieces. We have pieces for the smells or sights or other sensory information of a memory, the feelings associated with it, and the relational information. Then, usually while we sleep, our hippocampus, which has been keeping track of all those puzzle pieces, assembles them into a completed puzzle. The now completed puzzle is then stored in our long-term memory with similar puzzles that help it gain additional meaning for easier recall later. When we need the information again, our prefrontal cortex can go back into the *stacks* of our memory and get the puzzle and bring it out to consider and contemplate.

This is, fun fact, why cramming for a test all night is a whole lot less effective than cramming for a few hours and then sleeping. Your brain will use your snoozing to take all that information you just crammed about biology or seventeenth-century French literature and organize it in a way where you'll be able to recall—that is, access—this information during the test the next morning. If you don't sleep before the test, the information "puzzle pieces" can feel just out of reach, on the tip of your tongue and yet totally inaccessible to you.

This is one reason why sleep and naps are so important for kids. They're new humans in the world and therefore "cramming" information about the world, all day, every day. Without adequate, expected, and consistent sleep, that information doesn't get stored properly. The single best thing you can do for your kids' brain and mental health, from birth to twenty-five years old, is prioritize sleep.

OK, that's great, Jon, but what does this have to do with being triggered by your lack of personal differentiation from your kids?

We're getting there, I promise.

I've just described, in a simple, quick-and-dirty way, how memory works. But what about when it doesn't work the way we would like? What happens when we take in a memory before we have a developed prefrontal cortex, or when the prefrontal cortex is being shut out by the amygdala?

In short, we don't store these memories in the same way.

The most glaring example of this with adults is with "extreme trauma" memories. Regardless of when the extreme trauma occurs, when we are in a deeply traumatic situation, the brain does not organize and make meaning out of the sensory and emotional information in a clear way.[3]

In these moments, the brain is prioritizing survival. It wants to help us get through the next five minutes; it doesn't really care about being able to recall this stuff for the next five or fifty years. Also, if you're truly in a life-or-death situation (and not just having your amygdala hijacked), the sensory information can be incredibly disturbing or even painful. Your brain wants to protect you . . . even when the way it's protecting you has unintended consequences for you in the long term.

The result, in those extreme trauma cases, is often PTSD, post-traumatic stress disorder. In PTSD, the affected person's brain did not store the memory as a completed puzzle. As a result, the sensory and emotional information got stuck in limbo. The brain now has a bunch of puzzle pieces lying around. It knows that these pieces are related to something that needs to be remembered—in no small part because the event that they referenced was usually considered by the brain to be life-or-death. But because of the extreme trauma, the system scrambled the puzzle. At times, the sensory and emotional information can be almost impossible to recall. At other times, especially when the amygdala senses that the present conditions are similar enough to those at the time of the extreme trauma, they manifest as devastating unwanted intrusions.[4]

This is why a specific smell can send a survivor of sexual assault into a panic attack or why a loud sound can trigger flashbacks in a combat veteran.

To a lesser extent, those without diagnosable PTSD can have similar experiences with their traumatic memories. My dad died of small-cell bladder cancer in mid-August 2017. The entire experience, lasting a little over a year from the first symptoms, was *traumatic* for all of us. I am still processing it years later. For me, most of the last year of his life can be called "explicit memory"—in other words, a completed puzzle. But the week and day he died are still a sort of blur. I couldn't put it on a timeline like I can most nontraumatic memories. It's more like flashes, images, smells, feelings.

Every August now, without ever consciously being aware of it, my body *feels* it. I get distracted. I struggle to be empathetic to others. I am easily triggered. I am even more susceptible to symptoms of depression, a condition I do not typically struggle with. The memory, though not explicit, is still there, *implicitly* affecting me.

Childhood Memories

All of us have implicit memories from our childhoods.

When I was in grad school, one of my counseling professors told us about a case study of a child who was reacting to an implicit traumatic memory from the *first week of her life* as a newborn. She couldn't "remember" it, of course, but her limbic system, mostly formed at birth, had recorded the sensory information of this deeply disturbing experience. As a result, implicit memory of the extreme trauma was affecting her in adulthood as if it were something that had happened to her much later.

Other memories are implicit because the actions of your caregivers sent you into your fight-or-flight response. As a result, your brain internalizes them similarly to the way we store traumatic memories, and they aren't as easily accessible.

I was doing one-on-one counseling with someone a while back about their being triggered by their child refusing to put on their coat. I asked what the consequence of that behavior had been in their home growing up. (I ask this question all the time.)

The parent didn't remember ever refusing to put on their

coat so they assumed the punishment must have been pretty mild. We moved on. Then, months later, this person reached back out to me. They had asked their father about it and he had said nonchalantly that of course they had done that as a toddler and he had spanked them as a result.

This parent had blocked out those traumatic childhood memories. They represented violations of the parent-child relationship wherein their primary source of comfort and safety had intentionally harmed them. Now, in their mid-thirties, they were experiencing the shame, fear, and general discomfort of those experiences whenever their child refused to put on their coat.

This can and does happen, to some extent, to all of us.

We all have implicit memories, even if we weren't hit for our mistakes or defiance. We all have times when our parents punished us by shaming or yelling or otherwise sending us into our fight-or-flight response. Because of this, we remember, but not always explicitly. And the younger we were when it happened, the less we will remember explicitly.

Then, when our children—whom, as we have already established, we too often view as extensions of ourselves—do the stuff we used to do, the neural pathways associated with those old, often implicit memories fire back up.

It's no wonder so many of us are so triggered by our kids. There's no time in the mind, and our nervous system sometimes just flat out forgets that what is happening to our kids is not happening to us.

That's why when a parent comes to me and tells me their deepest frustration with their kids, it almost always is the very thing that is their own deepest vulnerable insecurity from childhood. It's a wound from their childhood—a fragmented memory of a time when their parents fell short of perfection and they learned, too harshly, that their whining, defiance, anger, or lying were a threat to their well-being or place in the family.

If you want to ensure your own kids grow up with all the same insecurities as you, make sure you shame or hurt them every time they do something that triggers *you*. That's one of the primary ways we pass down our flaws to the next generation. If, on the other hand, you want better for them and a healthier, more fulfilling life for you, you're going to have to learn to attend to personal differentiation.

Parental Projection and Autonomy

Another aspect of parents' failure to differentiate occurs when they attempt to live vicariously through their children.

When this happens, a parent projects not only their past shame and trauma onto their child's present reality, but also their unfulfilled dreams, desires, and aspirations. This can take many forms, some of which are significantly less obvious than you might expect.

When I talk about this and ask parents what they think I mean, they usually come up with scenarios from the media totally lacking in nuance. The elite college football player who has his career cut short by injury or a poor decision lives vicariously through his child who has the career the parent missed out on. The brilliant immigrant father who worked hard and was tough on his first-born child so she could have the career as a renowned doctor that he had so longed for.

In real life, the differentiation issues are often far more subtle.

A child shows interest in a field that their parent thinks is *"below them"* or is interested in a romantic partner who doesn't fit the picture of the person the parent *thought* they ought to be with. Or the child has a beautiful voice and a talent for theater even though it conflicts with their place on the basketball team their parent coaches . . . Wait. . . . That's just the plot of *High School Musical*.

An even more subtle form of this phenomenon is when a parent is triggered by their child simply expressing a difference of opinion. It can feel violating and disrespectful for your child to support a political candidate you disapprove of or to show interest in a religion that conflicts with your faith system.

The reason all these things may *feel* wrong to those of us who are still in the process of learning to foster healthy personal boundaries and differentiation is because we forget that our children are not simply extensions of us; they are full and whole persons, deserving of respect, dignity, and autonomy. Many parents' unconscious minds seem to forget that their children are distinct individuals, separate from them, and they deserve to be treated as such. Recognizing this fundamental truth is crucial in nurturing healthy parent-child relationships. It means acknowledging that children can and should have their own perspectives, preferences, and unique qualities that do not always align with those of their parents.

I think Dr. Shefali says it best in her groundbreaking book on conscious parenting, *The Conscious Parent: Transforming Ourselves, Empowering Our Children*:

> When you parent, it's crucial you realize you aren't raising a mini-me, but a spirit throbbing with its own signature. For this reason, it's important to separate who you are from who each of your children is. Children aren't

ours to possess or own in any way. When we know this in the depths of our soul, we tailor our raising of them to their needs, rather than molding them to fit our needs.[5]

When we are differentiated from our kids, they, in turn, get a kind, empathetic, compassionate, and attentive caregiver who doesn't get sucked into their messes but can instead be a firm anchor for them no matter the storms life brings.

We can't be that stable and secure presence if we're constantly being triggered by our children or getting pulled into their world by trying to live through them.

Consider this quote from the Harvard University Center on the Developing Child:

> Not all stress is the same. "Good stress" involves taking a chance on something one wants, like interviewing for a job or school, or giving a talk before strangers, and feeling rewarded when successful. "Tolerable stress" means that something bad happens, like losing a job or a loved one, but we have the personal resources and support systems to weather the storm. "Toxic stress" is . . . something so bad that we don't have the personal resources or support systems to navigate it, something that could plunge us into mental or physical ill health and throw us for a loop.[6]

The only difference between *tolerable* stressors, things that suck but don't ultimately do lasting damage to our kids, and *toxic* stressors, things that do lasting damage, is the presence of a stable support system. When we lack differentiation, we fail to be what our child needs to transform toxic stress into tolerable stress.

Unpacking Our Past

Once we fully embrace that our kids are not us, we also tend to get the most out of *our* parenting journey.

Many of our deep childhood wounds are lost to us for most of our adult life. Though these wounds often still affect us, we don't always know where those effects emanate from. As our children dredge up those implicit feelings and experiences, we have an opportunity, through the power of neural plasticity, to reprocess them explicitly and, in so doing, render them harmless.

Our brain's capacity to do this is what is leveraged in the most common established protocol for treating PTSD (though if you think you have PTSD or CPTSD, please consult a mental health professional for assistance before trying what I'm about to say). To work through a traumatic experience, victims have to learn to tell the story of the experience.

By bringing the puzzle pieces back to the forefront of the mind (while in a safe and controlled environment, like a therapist's office), the brain has another chance to store the memories in a less jumbled and confused way. This is why many trauma-informed therapists refer to going "through" the extremely traumatic experience rather than "getting over it."

When victims can finally tell the story of their trauma, including recalling the feelings associated with it, without being retraumatized by the broken memory, they effectively gain control over that memory by making it explicit.[7]

This new awareness and consciousness allows us to do exactly what Frankl outlines: to pause and respond rather than react.

Let me end this chapter by telling you how becoming a more conscious parent has changed my life.

Today, if I'm caring for myself well enough to be regulated and rational, when my kids trigger something in me, I look at it as an emotions detective. I do my best to get curious, not furious, and ask, "Why is this thing my kids are doing making me feel afraid, ashamed, or just flat-out mad?" Sometimes, it's nothing. I'm hungry or tired or the thing they're doing is just plain annoying. I chuckle and try to redirect them.

Sometimes, though, I realize I have no idea why what they're doing is so triggering. I take a few centering breaths and reach back in my mind and imagine myself as a child doing something similar. As I do so, I become consciously aware that there's nothing threatening me. The emotion begins to fade as I realize I am *safe* in my adult body. This is an incredibly helpful and grounding experience and has saved me from taking out my own unprocessed childhood issues on my kids more than a few times.

Other times, it takes processing with a trusted friend or even a few sessions with a journal before I can uncover why my body is reacting so viscerally to my kids. It can be exhausting work, but it's a small price to pay to gain the freedom Frankl speaks of.

I am no saint. I don't always remember to do it, believe me. The process of untangling your implicit childhood memories is a lifelong one. But the more times I work this "muscle," the stronger it gets. As I unpack each thing that triggers me—and through contemplative practices, reprocess them—my neural pathways respond to become more solidified.

When my kid does that triggering thing again and all I feel for them is empathy and understanding, that is when I know I am truly free.

8

Repair and Reconciliation

Reconciliation does not mean forgetting or trying to bury
the pain of conflict . . . reconciliation means working
together to correct the legacy of past injustice.

—NELSON MANDELA

What do we do when we don't act like the parents we hope to be? What do we do when our impulses get the best of us, when we lash out and punish or otherwise fail to live up to the (unachievable) perfect standard of parenting we see on social media and read about in parenting books? What can we do when we inevitably make mistakes?

The answer, we've established, cannot be to punish ourselves for those mistakes. Punishing yourself is no more effective than punishing your kids; neither brings positive results.

Instead, we have to learn to reconcile and repair what we rupture, being willing to extend to ourselves the same grace and forgiveness that we aspire to extend to our children. After all, we cannot give to our kids what we have not first learned to give to ourselves.

The uncomfortable truth is we, like our children, are all still very much works in progress. We're all still learning and growing. I am no exception. If many of you saw me parenting on my worst days out in public, you would never guess that I wrote this book. All of us will have days when we fall short of our own standards of parenting. All of us will have moments when we let the way we were conditioned—rather than our values—run the way we react. And as uncomfortable as it may be to accept, that is OK.

You are not defined by your worst parenting moments.

This is the first and often most difficult hurdle for those of us raised in punishment paradigms to get over. Many of you, having made it this far in the book, are hoping to kick punishment to the curb for good. You now realize that ensuring your child "feels bad enough" has little to do with growth or learning. Feeling ashamed and afraid is not the key to moral development or empathetic connection with peers or the world. Unkindness does not teach one to be kind. Disrespect does not teach one to be respectful. The question is, can you believe that about yourself too?

Many of us are our own worst critics. When we mess up, we get down on ourselves, mercilessly shaming and punishing ourselves for our mistakes and actions. Because we were raised on punishment, this self-flagellation feels necessary for change. We believe we must make ourselves feel bad enough to inspire ourselves to change. I urge you, stop. Stop believing that. Stop believing in the myth of punishment, even where it concerns you. Punishing yourself has nothing to do with creating positive lasting change. That myth is just the meaning you had to make out of the painful memory of experiencing punishment at the hands of the people you most loved.

You will make mistakes, and beating yourself up as penance will not help you become the parent you so desperately desire to be for your kids. The relentless pursuit to achieve parenting perfection is not good for us. All it proves is that we have yet to deconstruct the punishment paradigm where it concerns ourselves. In truth, hard as any of us might try, there is no avoiding all the mistakes in the game of parenting. And the good news is, even if we somehow could, being the perfect parent wouldn't be good for your kids either. . . .

As we've talked about throughout this book, kids learn as much or more from observing how we exist in the world as anything else. This is why it's impossible to become the parent you long to be without first learning how to reparent yourself; if you can't live the principles and values you're trying to instill in your children, there is just no way to effectively instill those values in any lasting way. It is perhaps this, above all else, that makes parenting the single hardest and yet most rewarding thing that most of us will ever do.

The Power of Mistakes

That said, the moments when you mess up and fail to live into your parenting values are, ironically, some of the most potentially positive and transformative parenting experiences you'll ever have. When we learn to embrace mistakes as opportunities for growth and learning and shepherd our children to do the same, the results can be astonishing. This is called adopting a "growth mindset."

The term "growth mindset" coined by Dr. Carol Dweck in her book *Mindset: The New Psychology of Success* is, at its core, the choice to believe that intelligence and skills are not "fixed" qualities. A person, through intentional hard work and perseverance, can "grow" beyond their current capacity especially by embracing failure, challenges, mistakes, and setbacks and choosing, in spite of those, to continue to grow.

Fixed mindset is exactly the opposite; it is choosing to believe that skills and intelligence are inherent, fixed qualities. To be clear, many people mistake "just trying harder" with having a "growth mindset." This is far from the truth. A growth mindset is less about *trying hard* and more about *how you view* your mistakes and setbacks.

The people I've worked with who have a fixed mindset (close to 50 percent if not more) don't really believe they have a capacity to grow from their mistakes and failures and therefore get down on themselves whenever they inevitably make a mistake. Mistakes, in the view of someone with a fixed mindset, are evidence of *character flaws,* not opportunities to learn. Those with fixed mindsets are, intentionally or not, choosing to contradict what we now know about the brain's ability to change and adapt (neural plasticity) and are often on a trajectory toward the pitfall of perfectionism we discussed earlier.

It's not entirely surprising that many parents today struggle with having a perfectionist or fixed mindset around parenting. One of the hallmarks of 1980s and 1990s parenting was the rise of near constant supervision and assessment.[1] Many of us were constantly watched and *assessed* in every aspect of life, from sports, to academics, and even artistic expression. As far as academics is concerned, there has, perhaps, never been a more tested generation than millennials. From the popularization of the SAT and ACT in the mid-twentieth century to "No Child Left Behind," which passed in 2001, most millennials, at least in the United States, took far more standardized tests than their parents or grandparents. Moreover, "No Child" put the burden on schools and teachers who could see consequences up to having their school closed as the result of their students' poor performance on standardized tests.

The result for many of us, and the generations since, was

the standardization of curriculum and the increased emphasis on doing things "the right way." Creativity and nonlinear thinking became secondary to obedience and compliance to the way we were being taught.

Today, valuing mistakes and failure as learning opportunities is foreign to so many children and parents. But if we can break free of that fixed way of thinking, the resulting change can be unimaginable.

Some years ago I had the opportunity to coach a girls' volleyball team and inadvertently wound up employing this mindset. They were high school freshmen, and they were . . . not great. These girls had tried out and been placed on the C team where their coach was . . . also not great. About halfway through the year, he was fired because of some personal issues, and I was brought in.

They had yet to win a single game.

The club director pulled me aside to tell me that she didn't expect or even care about their success, team or individual. None of these girls were on scholarship, and the C team cost a lot less to run than it brought in in club dues. She implied that these girls were never going to be any good. They were just there to keep the lights on for the one or two at the top who would grow six inches and play at Northwestern. Fixed mindset.

Given that I had just begun to learn about growth mindset, though not in such clear terms, and that one of my abiding core beliefs in life is that it's never too late, I took this as a challenge.

The thing I noticed immediately was that these girls were terrified of making mistakes. If they hit a ball into the net or served one out, even in practice, they would look at me and apologize. All eight of them were far more concerned about what their coach (their authority figure) thought of them than having fun, getting better, or even winning a game.

So I instituted a new policy.

Coach doesn't care about mistakes.

I never subbed a girl out or called a time-out to criticize them for making mistakes or even a series of mistakes (which was basically the standard practice for volleyball coaches at all levels). Instead, I reframed everything as a learning experience. Growth mindset instead of fixed mindset.

I also began to model what healthy processing of mistakes looked like. If I chose to start in a certain defensive position that hurt us, I would explain that it was my mistake and that now I know better. If I asked a girl to play a position or take on a task she was uncomfortable or unfamiliar with, I would take accountability. If I used all my time-outs and didn't have one when we really needed it, I would own it.

Soon, the girls started to mirror what I was modeling when they made mistakes on the court. They might say something like, "I could feel that my shoulders weren't squared up. That's why I missed," or, "I missed that serve long because I got greedy."

Over the next few weeks each of them began to trust their own ability to critically think, problem-solve, and make adjustments. Most important, they stopped trying to make me happy and began to lean into their own internal assessment of their performance. As a result, they made strides in performance well beyond what anyone expected. They even started to win, and not just a little.

Our season culminated in a second-place tournament finish (including winning a hard-fought match against the

B team girls who had been picked over them at tryouts) only a month or so after I had simply offered them the freedom to stop caring so much about what I thought.

If this were a Disney movie, you would have chalked it up to their having more fun, or you would see a training montage where they learned that defense is more important than offense . . . but it was so much deeper than that. Their success was born from *their own mindset shift* to trust their own perspective and experience and use it to innovate and think critically instead of defaulting to obedience to the adult in the room.

I was let go two weeks later when the *C* team was disbanded and the girls were pulled up to the higher-level teams. Those teams had started to struggle down the stretch, and the *C* team girls were so confident, optimistic, and, inexplicably, somehow now so talented that it became evident that their presence on the more competitive teams would be a huge boost. And it was.

Now, I'm not saying that this is always going to be the case. You're not always going to see massive competitive, academic, or achievement-based improvements when you start empowering your kids to move outside of a fixed mindset, but should that really be the goal anyway? These are the mindsets and neural pathways that lead to incredible *lifelong* resilience. What many parents seem to fail to grasp is that resilience, self-esteem, and a willingness to make mistakes and learn from them are far more important than a perfect SAT score or making the varsity team when our kids are sixteen. The goal for our kids and ourselves should be growth, not perfection.

Good Enough Parenting

Ever heard the aphorism "Perfect is the enemy of good"? It's especially true of parenting. As we already talked about in the chapter on modeling, perfection—and even *striving* for perfection—in parenting is self-destructive. It's not good for you, it's not good for your kids, and it lends itself to the exact antithesis of the growth we should be prioritizing.

That's not to say we shouldn't try to improve as parents. In fact, I doubt you would be reading this right now if you were totally uninterested in trying to improve as a parent. We just have to remember in the process that our goal is not perfection but *good enough* parenting.

Good enough parenting looks like giving yourself a break when you don't do things perfectly all the time. Some days they're going to watch two or five extra episodes of *Bluey*. Other days you'll reflect after bedtime and realize your kids ate nothing but granola bars all day. Still others you'll realize that you've been missing out on one-on-one time with your middle child for the last two weeks. In fact, typing this right now, I'm not exactly sure when I last gave my oldest a bath . . . I'm pretty sure this week . . . tonight I guess.

And what about all the "parenting tips" you've read about in this or other books or seen on social media? So many of us are convinced that if we don't have the right discipline script or if we praise our children in the wrong way or if we don't perfectly co-regulate them in their big feelings and snap and just yell at them instead, our mistakes will have lifelong consequences.

The truth is, none of these things, according to research, is actually going to lead to irrevocable harm to your child or their attachment to you as their caregiver. In fact, according to research into secure attachment in childhood, caregivers only needed to be "in sync" and attuned to their children's emotions 30 percent of the time to achieve secure attachment![2] Thirty percent! I go with advice from my friend Dr. Aliza Pressman, who offers us that if we can live into our parenting ideals "more often than not," we're good enough parents.[3]

I just want to take a moment to tell you as you read this, I don't just think you're a *good enough* parent, I think you're a truly *great* parent. The things we've covered are not easy. If you apply even 20 percent of what I've said so far and apologize when you don't, you're going to raise a resilient, compassionate, and whole person. So if you're worried that you don't measure up to what you see on social media or the *expectations* of parenting "experts," just know, you far exceed my expectations for the simple fact that you've made it this far.

You've got this. I believe in you.

Apologizing

If we're already *good enough* parents (not to say we can't all still improve) and we are going to employ a growth mindset for ourselves and foster the same in our children, how do we actually repair and reconcile when we mess up? Let me start with the best example of reconciliation I know.

In 1990, Nelson Mandela, having spent twenty-seven years in prison for his fight against apartheid, was finally released. (He did *not* die in prison, no matter what your memory says.) Four years later he would be elected president of South Africa. Apartheid was the deeply oppressive system in South

Africa that viciously enforced racial segregation and discrimination, inflicting unimaginable suffering and injustice upon the nonwhite population. For decades, apartheid divided the nation along the lines of skin color, denying nonwhite South Africans basic rights and liberties afforded to their white neighbors and subjecting them to violence and discrimination.

Mandela, one of the major leaders in the dismantling of apartheid, understood that for South Africa to truly move forward, it needed to confront its painful past and seek a path toward reconciliation rather than retribution and punishment. It would have been more than understandable for this man, unjustly incarcerated for more than a quarter of his life, to seek punishment for those responsible, but he chose what he deemed to be the better way.

And so Mandela conceived the Truth and Reconciliation Commission (TRC), a first-of-its-kind initiative that departed from traditional punitive models of justice employed for centuries throughout the world. The TRC's mission was not punishment, retribution, or revenge but rather truth, reconciliation, and healing. Its unique practices set it apart and make it a model of restorative justice to this day.

The TRC operated with unprecedented transparency, holding public hearings televised nationwide. Rather than focusing on the perpetrators, the *victims* were at the heart of the TRC's proceedings, sharing their stories and pain, and receiving acknowledgment and validation.

In a radical move, the TRC decided that the perpetrators could confess their crimes in exchange for amnesty from prosecution. The TRC meticulously documented testimonies, resulting in a comprehensive report that recommended primarily reparations and policy changes. Its aim was to unite a divided nation, simultaneously dismantling the legacy of apartheid while promoting inclusivity and healing.

These remarkable practices, under Mandela's visionary leadership, served as a testament to the transformational power of truth and reconciliation. Even in the face of immense suffering, the TRC demonstrated that forgiveness and healing were possible, setting an inspiring example for the world to follow, including us parents.

The two most essential things the TRC teaches us as parents are as follows:

First, the TRC highlights a truth that I've tried to underscore with this entire book, that punishment, whether through shaming, yelling, restricting, or otherwise hurting someone to attempt to get them to behave, is, in the long term, ineffective.

Second, that in order to adequately reconcile, you have to tell the truth and take accountability for the ways that you've harmed someone. That, in other words, the focus should be on the outcomes for the victim, not the intent of the perpetrator. Approach your children with the understanding that they are entitled to respect and dignity and hold yourself accountable for your actions.

Let me give you an example of what this looks like.

The last time I messed up and didn't live up to my ideals with my seven-year-old was—wait for it—thirty minutes ago. I fail to be a perfect parent at least once a day with at least one of my kids. In those cases I don't follow my own advice and wind up parenting (at worst) from my factory defaults. Stressed from work and life, trying to edit this book, running on too little sleep, and hungry for lunch an hour ago, I was already primed to blow. . . . And that was before my seven-year-old hit me in one of my biggest triggers.

"Stop it! Stop touching me!" cried the three-year-old.

"I'm not even touching you, I'm just standing here!" retorted his seven-year-old brother.

Which was true . . . or at least half true. Both of my older kids were supposed to be playing in the basement while I made lunch and their younger brother napped. While the seven-year-old wasn't "touching him," he had his little brother cornered on the stairs, blocking the path entirely so he couldn't get down to the basement, where his prized stuffed shark lay at the bottom of the stairs.

"Ouch!" yelled the three-year-old as he tried to push past and was pinned to the concrete wall. "You're pinching me!"

Suddenly, realizing he couldn't hold his brother back, the seven-year-old took two quick steps back, freeing his brother. Without hesitation the seven-year-old turned and sprinted down the stairs, snatching up the shark as he went past.

"Stop it right now! Stop picking on him!" My voice filled the air as my factory default parenting settings came online, triggered by my own depleted state and a little brother's utter helplessness. You see, I'm the youngest of three boys in my family of origin. I *hate* it when bigger siblings leverage their power like that.

I yell a lot less these days, but it still happens. The difference is in what happened next.

I stepped back, slamming my mouth shut before I could do more damage. I took a huge, oversized breath, in through my nose, held for a count of five, and out through my mouth.

You good, Dad? I asked myself. *Yes. Toddler first.*

In a stride I had my three-year-old in my arms. He buried his face into my shirt and started to speak totally incoherently about what had just happened. "I know. He blocked you and took your shark. It wasn't nice. I'm here."

We sat on the floor for probably a minute, me breathing deeply to regulate myself before engaging the seven-year-old. As my nervous system calmed down and I regained control, I felt my toddler in my arms begin to co-regulate and instinctively start to mirror my breathing.

When he was calm I stood and headed downstairs to my seven-year-old. Finding him on the giant beanbag chair, stuffed shark discarded, I knelt to his eye level and offered him an apology. "I yelled at you. I was frustrated and I blew up. That wasn't cool. I'm sorry."

Before I finish the story I want to take a moment to stop here and reflect on one of my major struggles in reconciliation and repair. It's taken me the better part of two years to stop finishing my apologies to my kids with "but," and it makes all the difference.

Cut the But

Many parents, both in the current generation and past generations, use apologies as Trojan horses for lectures, shame, or otherwise attempting to teach their children. Usually this goes something like this:

"I'm sorry that I yelled at you, *but* you really need to be more diligent about getting your schoolwork in on time. If you continue to not get your work in, your grades are going to suffer and you're not going to . . ." Or: "I'm sorry that I slapped you for talking back, *but* you really need to learn when to stop. You just make me so mad sometimes!"

Do you see how neither of these examples are really apologies? Sure, they use the right words at the beginning to sound like an apology, but ultimately they're not about taking accountability or responsibility for their harmful actions and seeking to repair with their child. These are Trojan horse apologies: manipulative rhetorical judo intended to lower the defenses of a child and open them up to receiving parental judgment and correction.

I doubt most parents have any idea that they're even doing this; I sure didn't. But I can tell you now that my factory default instincts are to include a "but" in the overwhelming majority of apologies I offer to my kids. It's a habit I'm working diligently to break.

The other issue with "but" apologies is that they often blame the parents' emotional response on the actions of the child. As we talked about in chapter 7, all of us have the ability to stop and reflect before acting on our impulses. This means that regardless of how your kids have triggered you, you have the capacity to not react emotionally. Of course you still will lose your cool at times—as I just demonstrated—but you always retain the agency to not lose it. This is empowering if you let it be, and it means, if you're thinking about blaming your kid for your own emotional reactions to their behavior, remember, this one is ultimately on you.

If you find yourself in the midst of an apology and have the overwhelming urge to say "but," just end the sentence and shut your mouth. In other words: *Cut the but*. It's a unique feature of the English language that anytime you're going to use "but" you've already constructed a coherent sentence. So quit while you're ahead. The word "but" too often erases everything before it, quickly turning apologies into assaults.

Back to the story.

My words hung in the air momentarily before the seven-year-old reacted.

"I just wanted a turn with the shark. It's not fair that he just gets to have it for the whole day when we just got it yesterday. I want to be able to play with it too, but if I ever have it, he tries to hurt me so I just have to run away!"

There was a lot of truth in what he said. Three-year-olds do get possessive with new things. They're in a phase of development where defining roles and possessions is a feature of their autonomy expression, but they usually still lack the ability to understand how that affects others. "My shark, your alligator" was how his little brother had been describing the two new stuffies, and there was no room for sharing in his current escalated (and admittedly *hangry*) state.

Rather than remind my oldest that he "got the alligator!" or say "But that's no reason to torment him!"—or even "Shut up, you know full well you don't care about this shark. You're just hungry and dysregulated and bored and looking for an outlet for your attention seeking because you were just in a hyperstimulating and overwhelming social environment, and now I'm ignoring you and you're picking on him to try and get your needs met"—I just said, "I know. He's little. It's like that sometimes. I'm sorry."

The urge to fill the awkward silence that followed was almost overwhelming, but I didn't. I just waited.

He continued to play, curled up with eyes down, with a tiny rubber band he found somewhere. Eventually he stood up, turned from me, and said, "That's okay." He walked upstairs and looked at his brother still sitting on the floor.

"Hey, Ollie, do you want to come play with the shark? I won't steal it again."

"OK!"

Giggles and shouts echoed up the stairs as I returned to the kitchen to make our long-awaited lunch.

Reconciliation and Repair

That's the power of being willing to prioritize the relationship over the parental hierarchy, connection over correction. Far from the "Say you're sorry right now!" approach of many parents, this is actually how you raise kids who will apologize to you, their siblings, and one day their spouses and children. Any apology given under the threat of punishment is just hollow lip service. On the other hand, when you model apologies, your kids will inevitably mirror them back to you.

Many of you might be thinking right now, "But your son didn't say sorry! That's not an apology!" That was me too. I was convinced that the word "sorry" was the only way to express remorse. You can see it in the way I apologized to him, both for my actions and the difficulty he has interpersonally with his brother because of his age. "Sorry" is in my apology DNA. But the truth is, apologies and the accountability they express are not less impactful because they lack the word "sorry." On the contrary, oftentimes, they are more sincere. Don't get me wrong, my kids absolutely still say "sorry" and I obviously do too; it's just not necessary.

He said two things that let me and his brother know he was seeking to repair. The first thing I want to highlight is that he offered that he wouldn't do the offending action again. That identifies that he not only knows it wasn't ideal, but that he's willing to *change his future behavior* accordingly. Second, he offered a place of reconnection, a helping of good connection to balance out the rupture.

That good relationship building after the fact does not undo the harm. Yelling at, shaming, or even putting your hands on your child cannot be undone with an apology or even positive connection. The only thing we can do is take accountability and change our actions going forward.

The reason there are so many parenting experts and social media creators out there who want to give you the perfect "apologizing to your kids script" (as a digital download for $17) is because many of us know apologizing is the *right* thing to do but so often we feel like we don't know the *right* way to do it.

Here's the good news. The way we repair with our kids is simple. As soon as you can, meet them where they are, own your mistakes, and learn from them. Then, focus on all of the amazing moments you have with them and realize the truth: In all likelihood, you're a great parent doing your best, *and your best is always enough.*

I say "as soon as you can" because the longer the rupture of a relationship lasts, the more difficult it is to eventually repair. Best practice is to repair as soon as possible. The sooner we can come back together after a period of disconnection, the less negative impact the disconnection tends to have.

This has proven to be true in my personal life as well. My parents undoubtedly had their disagreements growing up, often including yelling, but they also had a relationship rule to not go to bed angry. They didn't want to allow their relational ruptures to *fester.* Given that they were married for just short of forty-three years (and likely could have made it to over seventy years had my dad not died), I think it proved to be pretty good advice.

In every case that you can, repair as quickly as you can, taking accountability for your actions, truth telling, and offering that you will seek to do better in the future.

But what about those relational wounds from the past?

What about the things we've done, the ruptures that we've caused, that were left totally unrepaired? I want to ask you a question.

If your parents or a caregiver from your childhood called you up on the phone today to let you know by a strange coincidence they were reading this book and got to this section and realized that they didn't always do a good job of repairing when you were growing up—that they were calling you to let you know they were sorry that they didn't always handle your big emotions as well as they could have; that they often sought to correct rather than connect; that they were sorry for the inadvertent harm they caused through their "punish first, ask questions never" paradigm; that, in other words, if they could go back and parent how I have proposed we parent in this book, they would—would you think it was too late to matter?

We always have an opportunity to repair.

Don't get me wrong, words will not be enough. Action will be required. If my son had attempted to repair his relationship with his brother through words, only to take the stuffed shark again and run off to his room, it likely would have been even more of a rupture.

Similarly, if you're reading this chapter and thinking that it negates everything else in this book; that the ability to "say sorry" will then give you license to just go on parenting however harmfully and ineffectively you want and just "fix it later," you've missed the point. Our best is always enough, but when we inevitably do fall short and fail, we have a unique *opportunity* to grow even deeper in our relationship with our children. That's what I call the failure relationship paradox.

The Failure Relationship Paradox

I learned about this paradox not in counseling courses but actually in business school. It's a customer relations principle. Fixing a problem a customer had with your company or product is paradoxically *better* than the customer never having the problem in the first place.

I recently experienced this on a United Airlines flight. United is one of these airline companies that is so big, with so many flights, it's hard to imagine them caring about one passenger. They don't have a reputation for being particularly luxurious like British Airways, or particularly cheap like Spirit, or even particularly fun like Southwest. They are, admittedly, a little boring. They come in the middle of the pack for reliability, comfort, price, and general customer satisfaction. But because I live in Chicagoland, home of O'Hare International Airport where United has been top dog for my whole life, I've often flown United.

Flying with three kids, including two toddlers, is exhausting. One of our absolutely must-have items that makes flying more manageable is our huge double stroller. It allows us to load up the bottom with our junk and strap our two younger kids in while we race through the terminal, often a little later than we planned on being. Basically every U.S. airline gate-checks your stroller for free and has it ready for you on the jet bridge when you deplane. Imagine my horror when, after exiting the plane on our United flight to Orlando, one of the tiny detachable adapter arms, essential to the stroller's functionality, was missing.

My stress response flared. I was suddenly in a panic. How would we navigate an unknown airport with three kids and a broken stroller?! And what about after that? Our trip included several days of heavy walking, and there was no way our two-year-old and three-year-old would be able to keep up.

I was left standing on the jet bridge, stroller in pieces in my hands, as the flight attendants and baggage handlers all finished their tasks and left. I was alone, standing there with a broken stroller, and my wife with three kids (one of whom just missed his nap) waiting in the terminal for me to bring the stroller.

The last person to leave the plane was the pilot himself. "Need something?" he asked with a smile.

"Uh, my stroller is missing a piece. I don't know if it's back in Chicago or under the plane or it fell into someone else's luggage or what."

"Do you have a picture of what it looks like?"

"Uh, hang on," I said, taking the identical piece off from the reverse side and handing it to him.

"All right, let me see what I can do."

To my shock, rather than hopping on a radio or calling for customer service, he walked out the door on the jet bridge, down the stairs to look for the piece himself. I stood there, eyes wide, imagining this pilot in his full pilot's uniform who had just flown several hundred people several hundred miles crawling into the cargo hold.

Minutes later he returned, the stroller piece I had given him still in hand, now joined by its partner. With a smile he handed them over as I thanked him profusely.

"Not a problem. Happy to help."

Now, I'm not endorsing any airline in this book, nor do I even know this pilot's name. What I will say is that experience has left me with an entirely different perspective on United. My begrudging relationship with the airline I used only because of my proximity to its base of operations was totally transformed.

Was I upset that the carelessness of some other employee had meant I almost lost my stroller? No, of course not. I was focused on the fact that the pilot had *made it right*.

This is the failure relationship paradox.

Just like how we learned in chapters 4 and 5 that getting a question wrong on a test is *more* effective for learning the material, and falling off the playground equipment when you're young means you're *less* likely to get more hurt later on, getting it "right" all the time in your relationships isn't what leads to the deepest connections. On the contrary, it's what we do when we get it wrong that does that. Our deepest connections are forged in the crucible of rupture and repair.

This is why, spoiler alert, every sappy romance movie has that scene about an hour and five minutes in where the couple *almost* calls it quits. Where the guy finds out she's been trying to get him to dump her for ten days, or the girl finds out that he was only with her in the first place because of a bet. We intrinsically know that we need the moments of disconnection for the connection to feel permanent.

And that's the silver lining here before we end with some practical strategies. How you repair with your kids is not only essential for teaching growth mindset and raising kids who know how to repair themselves; it's also going to be the very thing that deepens your forever connection to your tiny human.

The WHOLE Parent Method

Welcome to the heart of this book, where theory transforms into practical action.

The journey so far has been about self-discovery and establishing a new foundation for your parenting. Now it's time to take that knowledge and put it into practice, day in and day out. The 5-Step WHOLE Parent Method is not just a set of guidelines; it's a transformative process that will revolutionize your relationship with your child and your own emotional well-being based on the brain-based principles we've already covered.

The method uses the acronym WHOLE, a mnemonic device with each letter representing a specific step you can use in some of the most difficult parenting moments. The goal of this method is to give you an actionable, step-by-step plan of exactly what to do when you find yourself in those moments of parenting where the rubber meets the road. These tend to be the moments when we are most likely to *feel* like punishment is the best or only option. Now, you're going to have WHOLE function as your new alternative paradigm.

Each step of this method is clear, easy to implement, and, unlike punishment, highly effective. The steps work with your child's brain and development instead of against it, for better long-term results and connection. These steps will enable you to navigate the challenges of parenthood with grace and understanding, creating a supportive and nurturing environment for both you and your child.

As we explore each step, you'll discover how to connect more deeply with your child, respond to their needs in ways that fosters trust and security, and navigate the ups and downs of parenting with newfound confidence. This is where theory and knowledge translate into real-world action, where you'll see immediate changes in your interactions with your child.

Don't get me wrong, the five steps of the WHOLE Parent Method are not a magic one-size-fits-all solution or cure for misbehavior; the method is a flexible framework that can be tailored to your unique family dynamics and circumstances. It is meant to adapt and evolve as your child matures and as your relationship deepens.

So as we dive into the practical and actionable WHOLE Parent Method, prepare yourself for a journey of transformation and growth. This has the power not only to enhance your parenting skills but also to bring a sense of fulfillment and joy to your role as a parent.

9

Consider the Wiring

One of the things I learned in first responder training was the importance of assessing a situation and environment before attempting to provide aid.

"Whenever you arrive on the scene, your first job is to stop, breathe, and become aware of your surroundings," the trainer told us. I was in high school at the time, and the training has since not amounted to anything in my professional or personal life, but I remember that idea vividly. I think it was because *stopping and assessing* instead of jumping into action felt so counterintuitive.

The trainer went on to tell horror stories of paramedics and other first responders rushing into situations without pausing first to assess. One rushed to an unconscious person on the ground and was electrocuted by a downed power line they hadn't noticed; another got too close to the edge of a cliff and wound up falling off. In these situations, the responders had engaged in a phenomenon the trainer called "tunnel vision."

In an effort to help, they blocked out or ignored essential information, and as a result the tragedy was compounded. I remember clearly one example where a bystander assumed a woman lying on the ground was seriously injured when, in fact, she was mostly fine; in their haste, the person trying to help her was hit by a car and killed. Almost two decades later I remember these stories as a dire warning to stop and take in the scene before you run in to help.

We as parents often have the same inclination toward tunnel vision. We are frequently faced with situations that trigger our survival instincts, feelings of shame, or factory default parenting. Too often, we just go barreling into the dysfunction. Sometimes we hurt ourselves in the process, but more often we resort to punishment and make everything worse.

That's why step 1 of the WHOLE Parent Method is to stop and consider the Wiring.

The Wiring I'm talking about here has a double meaning. It refers to the neural pathways and development of both your brain *and* your child's brain. It's about examining the assumptions your brain is making about the situation because of the way you and your child are "wired." If you don't stop and consider wiring first, you're going in blind. To solve any problem, you first must know what the problem is. This is why the first thing I talked about in this book after the ineffectiveness of punishment was curiosity. To effectively "Consider the Wiring," let's break this step into three sub-steps.

First, Do No Harm

The first sub-step is simple: "First, do no harm." If your kids are playing with the stove or holding a kitchen knife, the absolute first thing you have to do is prevent major harm. Walk over to them calmly and (physically if necessary) help them come into a safe, boundaried space. The same goes if they're running toward a busy street. While I am a firm believer that physical force is never a solution to behavior issues, I have basically tackled my kids (and given them permission to tackle their younger siblings) if they're going to get hit by a car.

This seems almost too obvious to state in those early childhood scenarios, but the same goes for later problems. If your older child is presenting a credible threat of self-harm or suicide, you call 911. If you find out that they are sick or injured as the result of drugs or some other foolish decision, your primary job becomes keeping them safe and getting them help. It's never OK to let your kid "find their own way home" as a form of consequence if they get intoxicated at a party. I've known too many parents who foolishly skipped out on this responsibility and had catastrophic consequences as a result.

Self-Check

After ensuring that no serious harm is going to come to anyone involved, it's time to move on to sub-step two. This is where you have to consider and consciously become aware of your thoughts, impulses, and even physiology. This process is called mindfulness, introspective self-awareness, metacognition, or "thinking about thinking." Metacognition, especially when your amygdala is trying to drive, takes practice to master. None of us are born experts in this. On the contrary, this is one of those skills that takes years of development and practice to hone. The good news is, because of neural plasticity, we know that we can physically change our brains to make mindfulness practices easier (and even automatic) through repetition.[1] My ability to practice metacognition is still very much a work in progress, and often it takes another adult in the room (usually my wife) intervening before I realize that I need to take a breath. Ultimately the goal is being able to instinctively pause and respond rather than react. Said differently, we need to learn to stop before we engage, and go, "Wow, I'm feeling really triggered by this situation. I need to get myself under control before moving forward."

Things to consider in your own metacognition process are:

- What is my body doing right now? Am I breathing fast? Are my muscles tense? Are my fists or jaw clenched? Is my temperature rising? Am I in survival mode?
- Are my basic needs being met (HALT, and so on)?
- Why do I feel angry or frustrated? Would I have been shamed or punished for this as a child? Is my frustration really about my kids, or something else? Am I really just feeling disappointed or sad?
- Do I have a plan to work through this situation, or am I just reacting in the moment?
- Am *I* in a good place to teach right now?

It is this last question that really must be answered before you move on to the next. Remember, it is a myth that you have to address problematic situations in the moment, beyond preventing immediate serious harm. Not everything is an emergency that must be dealt with in the moment. In fact, most things are better dealt with once you're calm and collected.

Their Wiring

The third sub-step is considering your kid's brain and what's happening there. Oftentimes this is much easier after you've engaged in mindfulness yourself. This is because along with other grounding exercises, mindfulness is an extremely effective therapy tool for getting your prefrontal cortex back online and in control.

Once you're in a "responsive" state of mind rather than a "reactive" state of mind, you can begin to ask many of the same questions you asked about yourself, only this time about your child.

- What is their body doing right now?
- Does it feel like they're dysregulated or in survival mode?
- Which part of the behavior triangle is this coming from? Is it possible they're hungry, angry, lonely, or tired (HALT)? Which need are they trying to get met (Maslow's stairs)?
- What is the developmental backdrop? Are they aware of what they're doing? Are they in control of their emotions and actions right now? What's the subtext of what's going on here?
- Are they in a good place to learn right now?

Some of these are going to be really hard to answer with certainty. No two kids are identical, and their developmental considerations specifically can be challenging to know. With my own kids, I've witnessed firsthand how "two and a half years old" can mean three entirely different things developmentally. The simplest thing to keep in mind is that their brain's ability to regulate their emotions, based on their physical brain anatomy, is still way behind what you have as an adult. So much of their maturity is just going to come with time.

That said, even if you're not an expert on child development or behavioral psychology, you *are* an expert on *your* child. The most important question here is, "Are they in a good place to learn right now?" If they aren't in a receptive state, your discipline isn't going to be effective. You are the best one to assess that. Trust yourself.

Remember that the goal of the WHOLE Wiring step is for you to assess the situation, prevent immediate serious harm, check in with yourself, and consider what's going on with your child's brain. If you do those things first, you're going to be well on your way to engaging your child effectively instead of just reacting and punishing.

10

Honor the Experience

The second step in engaging your child without punishment, once you've considered the Wiring, is to <u>H</u>onor their experience and emotions. I've broken this step down into two parts as well.

Heart-to-Heart

The first part of Honoring is to, regardless of the circumstances, engage your child first with connection. I think the majority of communication breakdowns that happen between parents and children of all ages can be chalked up to a failure to connect first. Here's what that might look like:

- When your child runs up to you crying, you bend down and pick them up.
- When they're not getting off their tablet, you place a hand on their shoulder until you·have their eyes.

- When they come home devastated by the end of a high school romance, you show your concern and embrace them (even if the relationship was only three days long).

I am singularly confident that this one piece of advice alone is worth a thousand times more than you paid for this book, regardless of whether your child is thirty years old or has yet to be born. When we fail to connect "heart-to-heart" before we attempt to communicate brain-to-brain, any advice we give will ring hollow, the boundaries we set will feel impersonal, and the discipline we attempt to institute will prove ineffective. In fact, you can do everything else in this book, but if you fail to lead with connection, you're likely going to feel like something is still off.

We humans are first and foremost emotional, not logical, and trying to appeal to the logic of an emotional person (and especially an emotional adolescent) before connecting with them will almost always lead to your child shutting you out. When we get shut out, we often then get triggered and say some variation of, "Fine, if you're not going to talk to me, you're grounded for a week!"

The reason humans are not primarily logical creatures but are first and foremost emotional is because the evolutionarily older structures in our brain—the brainstem and limbic system, those parts that are activated in survival mode—are much *faster* than our neocortex (the logic part). Because the part of our brain responsible for emotions is *faster*, it reacts more quickly than the part of our brain responsible for logic. Frequently, what we are doing as humans is encountering things that trigger our emotions and then rationalizing those emotions moments later. Adults who have a fully developed prefrontal cortex can, in most cases, override their initial emotional reaction, meaning their emotions have less of an ability to hold them totally hostage.

Not so for your tiny or even teenaged human. The path to getting them regulated and in a receptive brain state always traverses *through* their feelings. Meeting them in their feelings by leveraging yours is called "limbic resonance." If you try to bypass connection and begin with correction, direction, or especially punishment, you will run into a brick wall and often wind up feeling helpless. Even if punishment wasn't your initial reaction, often when we feel helplessness, we reach for control by resorting to punishment . . . which further triggers your child and makes things much worse.

That's why you really cannot miss this step and still be successful.

Connection can look different based on the age, stage, and personal characteristics of your kids. Some kids don't like to be hugged, for instance. Others just need to be listened to while they rant. Again, you are the expert on your kid, and if you're unsure, just ask them (preferably *not* when they're highly emotional).

One tip that seems to always work with younger kids is to meet your child at or below their eye level. Standing over a kid can actually trigger their stress response, while meeting them eye to eye and embracing them releases calming hormones into their brain to regain stasis.[1]

Validation

The second part of honoring their experience is in how we engage *during* that connection. Once we connect heart-to-heart we need to acknowledge and validate. Human beings have a fundamental need to feel seen, heard, and valued, regardless of their emotional state. When parents try to ignore the emotions of their child or redirect them too quickly without validation, it can have the same effect as failing to connect altogether. On the other hand, by helping your child to accurately label and accept their feelings, you both guide them to a place of regulation and help to build regulation neural pathways for the future.

Start by mirroring back to your child what you observe. Verbalize and label the emotion your child is *likely* feeling and then wait for confirmation.

For instance, if your child seems or is visibly upset about leaving the park, a simple acknowledgment like "I can see that you're upset about leaving the park right now" helps to determine if, in fact, that is what's going on. Their prefrontal cortex is not driving during a meltdown. They are in survival mode and are actively seeking out new threats. By simply positioning yourself as a person trying to understand and help— someone on their team and working toward a goal with them—you can begin to move them back to a regulated state.

You're not just parroting back their emotions to make them feel better either. You're also providing them with the language tools they might not yet possess. As Dr. Aliza Pressman aptly states, "Helping your [child] name their feelings—and by extension learn to recognize them—can communicate to toddlers that those intense feelings are normal."[2]

Dan Siegel and Tina Payne Bryson call this strategy "Name It to Tame It" in their bestselling book *The Whole-Brain Child*:

> To tell a story that makes sense, the left brain must put things in order, using words and logic. The right brain

contributes the bodily sensations, raw emotions, and personal memories, so we can see the whole picture and communicate our experience. This is the scientific explanation behind why journaling and talking about a difficult event can be so powerful in helping us heal. In fact, research shows that merely assigning a name or label to what we feel literally calms down the activity of the emotional circuitry in the right hemisphere.[3]

Honoring emotions in this way is not about finding an immediate solution or diminishing the intensity of what your kids are feeling, even if that is a by-product. That's where most parents get off track trying to help their kids get back to a regulated state. It's simply taking the deliberate step, up front, to say, "I hear you. I understand. Here's what that sounds like to me."

By validating through naming and labeling emotions, we give our children a way to express and understand what they're feeling. We are modeling to them and, in fact, directly helping them become emotions detectives who introspectively get curious about what they are feeling rather than dismissing or avoiding it.

For a child who is throwing a tantrum because they can't have a piece of candy, you might say, "It seems like you're feeling really frustrated about not having the candy." Speaking to kids in this way doesn't mean that you should immediately give them a piece of candy because they're frustrated (even though that's what many critics of punishment-free parenting seem to assume we all do). On the contrary, validating your child's feeling of disappointment around not having candy can help equip your child to build frustration tolerance in the moment and in the long term.

This step is all about parenting in such a way as to provide a safe space where children's emotions are recognized, acknowledged, and understood. By naming and validating their feelings, you're laying the groundwork for deeper communication and understanding in the subsequent steps.

Honoring, at its core, looks like learning to trust your kids: trusting them to have big feelings without distracting them or rescuing them and trusting them when they communicate how they feel or perceive the world. It's about trusting them enough to say, "I see that you're hurting, and I'm here in it with you." This is important not only because it helps our kids feel seen, heard, and valued, but also because when we trust our kids they learn to trust themselves. Empowering your kids by honoring their emotions and teaching them to trust in their own intuition is among the most profound gifts you can give them as a parent, leaving an enduring mark on their journey to self-discovery and unbreakable resilience.

11

Outline the Boundary

"I know you're mad at me right now, and it's totally OK to be mad. I can't let you hit me or your brother in the face with a baseball bat."

The number of times I have had to say some variation of that phrase is far too great to count. You read a similar, more protracted exchange about bike helmets in chapter 5.

Without going back over all the reasons that boundaries are important, we can acknowledge that some of the hardest times to hold empathetic boundaries are in the moments of dysregulation. Even so, the third step in WHOLE is Outline the Boundary.

Many well-meaning parents give in on boundaries not out of honest reconsideration and flexibility (both positive parenting attributes), but rather because they are worn down by incessant whining or badgering. This conditions kids to believe that they are in control of the boundaries and therefore, ultimately, the boundaries don't really exist.

The best rule of thumb is, if you truly feel comfortable changing a boundary based on the insistence of your child, perhaps that boundary was in the wrong place.

An easy exercise is to use something unreasonably extreme: I like to use the example of playing with a chainsaw. You wouldn't let your child play with a chainsaw no matter how much they whined or badgered you. If they tried to do it anyway, you would hold that boundary. If you felt that the boundary still could not be respected, you would put the chainsaw in a place where the child could not have access to it. If they were able to find it or get access anyway, you would eventually have to lock it up in a safe or choose to get rid of it and be forced to hire out any jobs that required the use of a chainsaw.

It might be that once your child reached a certain age and was adequately trained in using the tool, you might change the boundary to allow them to access the chainsaw under certain circumstances. But there is no scenario where you would simply *let* your child play with it just because they badgered you.

That's a boundary in a nutshell.

When your child is dysregulated, the key is to outline that boundary and the consequences—both natural and logical—of violating the boundary. Outlining a boundary before connecting and being regulated yourself and explicitly validating their perspective (wiring and honoring) will be significantly less effective. You have to meet them heart-to-heart first, then you can state and hold the proper boundary to ultimately keep them, and others, safe.

That said, kids who are upset often need to have well-established boundaries outlined. When they get into this different brain state, they can get incredibly impulsive and are more likely to violate even well-established boundaries.

This really shouldn't be surprising to any of us. Think about the resolutions we set up for ourselves that we often fail to uphold when we're dysregulated:

- I am not going to yell at my kids anymore.
- I am not going to eat "junk" food.
- I'm going to start working out at the gym.
- I'm going to get up early every morning.
- I'm not going to argue politics with extended family on Facebook.

I would like to say this last one is just me but . . . let's be real. It's a lot of us. When we get into reactive brain states that don't center on long-term decision making, our best resolutions become incredibly difficult to uphold. This is why firefighters drill and drill their protocols and practices *before* a fire. Their work has to become so second nature to them that even when their brain goes into full-on survival mode in a burning building, they still stick to doing things by the book.

The same is true for us and our kids. It is absolutely essential to outline boundaries during moments of deep dysregulation until those boundaries keeping them safe become second nature to them later in adolescence. Until then, we will keep outlining.

Outlining the boundary is really not that complicated a process compared to the first two steps in the WHOLE Parent Method, but it still needs to be tailored to any given situation.

If you're looking for a script, here's one. Learn it well enough that you can do it without thinking and then chuck it out and adapt on the fly.

State the Issue: I understand that you are feeling [insert labeled feeling] because you want to [insert behavior].

Empathize: I sometimes get [insert labeled feeling] too.

Validate the Feeling: It is OK to feel [insert feeling].

Outline the Boundary: I cannot let you [insert behavior] because [insert rationale].

If you plan on imposing a consequence as a teaching tool if they violate the boundary, tack on the following:

Define the Consequence: If you [insert behavior] I am going to have to [insert consequence] to keep you safe.

I'll give you a much more realistic example than the chainsaw one I used earlier—one many of us will run into in early adolescence:

I understand that you are **disappointed** because you want to **have an Instagram profile.** I sometimes get **disappointed** about things I want to do that I can't do too. It's OK to feel **frustrated with me about it.** I cannot let you **download Instagram** because **even though I trust you, I truly believe that thirteen is too young for an Instagram. We can talk more**

about that if you want to understand our decision further. If you **choose to download Instagram** anyway, I am going to have to **switch you back to your old flip phone** to keep you safe.

Once you outline the boundary, you can *finally* move to the two problem-solving phases of the WHOLE Parent Method.

12

Lead Them Out

Finally we get to the step in the WHOLE Parent Method, Lead Them Out, where most people attempt to *begin* . . . to their peril. Once we have considered the larger context (wiring), established a connection with our kids to validate their experience (honor), and stated and maintained the boundary (outline), we can begin problem solving.

But wait—don't start barking out orders or suggestions quite yet. If you're truly interested in the best long-term flourishing and resilience for your kids, here are the two reasons why you should pause here and give them some space.

Dare to Wait

When our kids are experiencing a lot of complicated or even uncomfortable emotions (that we just helped them identify and label), we have an invaluable opportunity to help them build up some emotional *tolerance*. Emotional tolerance, especially for the most uncomfortable emotions like grief, anguish, and anger, is not fun to build or have to watch your children build . . . but it is crucial to long-term emotional health and well-being. In fact, it's usually the lack of emotional tolerance that manifests as the good and bad emotions bucket system. For many of us, our parents' emotional *intolerance* caused them to shame, punish, or ignore us when *we* were having uncomfortable feelings, modeling to us that a lack of emotional tolerance is desirable or at least typical.

The problem is, it's really hard to be an emotions detective when you're also intolerant of uncomfortable feelings. So instead, many of us—and men especially—just lash out rather than having to sit in the challenging feelings.

Emotional tolerance is like any muscle. The more time you spend stretching and pushing it, the stronger and more flexible it becomes. This is the *real* way to "toughen up your kids for the real world." Dare to wait *before* offering to save them from their feelings.

The second reason to give your kids some space is that when you wait before leading, you actually give them the opportunity to lead themselves. Throughout this book I've been talking about how the best parents ultimately discipline themselves out of a job. Similarly, the best parents also make space to become *unnecessary* in aspects of their children's lives. So many parents are so eager to save their kids from minor emotional bumps and bruises that they ultimately give them far less autonomy than they need . . . and make them a lot less resilient as a result.

One of the things I've learned from strength training is that people often get the most out of their workout in the last few reps when they're struggling.

Waiting to let your kids struggle a bit in those big feelings is like a personal trainer giving you an extra moment to push that last rep before bailing you out. So too with kids. Learning to lead themselves out of their big feelings is immeasurably more beneficial than having you lead them out. So give them a chance. Be secure enough to let them struggle. Once you wait a minute and let them sit in their big feelings to give them the opportunity for that growth, *then* (finally) we can lead them out.

Leading Through the Storm

During my seminary education I spent significant time studying leaders and leadership. I've learned many things about effective communication and social science that have helped me become a better parent. But one concept stands above the rest.

The best leaders—in business, politics, athletics, and more—all understand that in order to achieve the best results, everyone has to win. In his perennial bestseller *The 7 Habits of Highly Effective People,* Stephen Covey argues that most of us have been indoctrinated from a young age into a "Win/Lose" paradigm. This is fundamentally a scarcity mindset: *There is not enough to go around, and so in order for me to win, others have to lose.* Approaching leadership, discipline, regulation, or really anything in parenting from a scarcity mindset, especially one where in order for you as a parent to "win," your child has to lose, will almost always result in failure.

The alternative way of thinking, according to Covey, is called "win-win thinking." He writes:

Most people tend to think in terms of dichotomies: strong or weak, hardball or softball, win or lose, but that kind of thinking is fundamentally flawed. It's based on power and position rather than on principle. Win/Win is based on the paradigm that there is plenty for everybody, that one person's success is not achieved at the expense or exclusion of the success of others.[1]

He goes on to warn against the default "lose-win" thinker:

Lose/Win people bury a lot of feelings. And unexpressed feelings come forth later in uglier ways. Psychosomatic illnesses often are the reincarnation of cumulative resentment, deep disappointment and disillusionment repressed by the Lose/Win mentality. Disproportionate rage or anger, overreaction to minor provocation, and cynicism are other embodiments of suppressed emotion. People who are constantly repressing, not transcending feelings toward a higher meaning find that it affects the quality of their relationships with others.[2]

If reading this paragraph in the context of parenting just hit you like a freight train . . . yeah, me too.

A lot of this goes back to our cultural value for children to be obedient. Win-win mindsets don't fit for those who think the goal of parenting is to force their child into submission and gain total compliance.

If, on the other hand, you, like me, see your role as a parent as primarily a life consultant and "regent," helping your child prepare for adolescence and adulthood by giving them tools and strategies while keeping them safe, then embodying a win-win mindset is going to help guide you in the right direction.

The ultimate goal of effectively leading your child through

their emotional storms is to assist them in moving back into a regulated state through modeling, grounding exercises, and other tools.

This can look a lot of different ways. In fact, compared with the other three steps you've already learned and the one coming next, this step has the most variability. It would be impossible for me to give you all of the different ways you will need to choose to lead because they will be tailored to every unique situation and to your unique children. Here are a few, grounded in neuroscience, that I have found work for my kids and the kids of the parents I help.

Some "Leading" Techniques to Try

Silliness is an effective way to lead many kids out of unhelpful sympathetic stress loops. My three-year-old, for example, is one such kid and has been since he was about one. Silliness is a tool that is exactly what it sounds like. You act a little silly. How does it work? Laughter can have a profound impact on mood by releasing endorphins and decreasing stress-making hormones.[3] It works for many of us and, for my three-year-old, a classic little bit of slapstick can really help him reset.

Sing it is another tool I like to offer parents (and one that happens to work well on my youngest). "Sing it" leverages the profound power music has on our brains to help us communicate even when a child is totally dysregulated. As we've talked about, when a child is melting down, their emotional center (limbic system) is overwhelming them and their logic center (prefrontal cortex) has to take a backseat. Music can be a tool in these moments because it actually has the ability to cut through and impact *both* our logic and emotional centers simultaneously, allowing your kid's brain to reintegrate.[4] What this means is, communicating through song, *singing* your message, can totally change your child's ability to hear and receive what you're trying to say.

Grounding is what I recommend most of the time for older kids. Grounding is a term from the therapy/psychology world that refers to a set of tools (primarily for adults) that help them cope with overwhelming or high-stress situations. Similar to "sing it," these are tools designed to help us reactivate different areas of our brain to calm us down and move us out of our fight-or-flight sympathetic nervous response. The most popular grounding exercise is five, four, three, two, one, where an overwhelmed person methodically names five things they can see, four things they can feel, three things they can hear, two they can smell, and one they can taste. For kids, I modify this by simply asking them to name six things they can see and their color. I can't tell you the number of parents who I've worked with who say that this tool totally changed their life during meltdowns, turning what were previously thirty-minute-plus tantrums into three-minute grounding exercises.

Centering breaths is perhaps the most basic tool of all. Centering breaths, or vagal breathing, can be done a number of ways, but I'll offer the two I utilize. First, and most commonly, you breathe slowly and intentionally, in through your nose, holding for a beat, and out through your mouth like you're blowing bubbles. Alternatively you can breathe in for a count of five, hold for a count of four, and out, slowly, for a count of eight. For kids, simply refocusing on just breathing slowly is usually enough.

The second way to do vagal breathing is by implementing a "big sigh." A big sigh is exactly what it sounds like. Take in a deep breath of air and let it all fall out of you, relaxing your shoulders, head, and neck as you do. The reason these types of breathing are effective is they stimulate the tenth cranial nerve called the *vagus nerve,* one of the fundamental pieces of the parasympathetic nervous system designed to calm us down when we get overwhelmed or stressed out. Stimulating the vagus nerve chills us out, and, yes, it works on both kids and adults.

In order to figure out which one of these tools works well on your kids, you'll need to do some trial and error as well as some adaptation. Remember, *you* are the expert on your child and thus are a way better leader for them than I am. These are just some places to start and tools to test out on your path to win-win punishment-free parenting.

13

Empower for the Future

As we reach the end of the WHOLE Parent Method framework, we refocus on our long-term goals for our kids. Above all else, <u>E</u>mpower for the Future is about long-term *mindset*. Punishment-based parenting techniques often feel like trying to play Whac-A-Mole with problematic behaviors. . . . Punishment-free parenting is how we raise our kids to self-discipline for the long term.

Setting aside the short term for the long term is about understanding our place in the growing process of the humans we have the incredible opportunity to raise.

Becoming a Guide

One of my fundamental parenting mindset shifts came when I tied parenting to the work of Joseph Campbell and his distillation of the *Hero's Journey*.

Even if you don't know anything about it, you've seen it played out a hundred times. A hero is born when a seemingly ordinary person is called to an adventure. Initially they refuse the call but finally, with the help of a mentor, they are pushed beyond the threshold of normal life into an extraordinary world. What follows are tests of their strength, resilience, and fortitude until eventually they overcome. Whether it's Luke Skywalker, Frodo Baggins, Harry Potter, Neo from *The Matrix,* Simba from *The Lion King,* or Cady Heron from *Mean Girls,* the contexts might be different but the bones of the story are almost always the same.

Unsurprisingly, people, including parents, often see themselves as the heroes of their own stories. Psychologically speaking, all humans are, at our core, egocentric to some degree. Ideally we grow out of this as our brains develop, but we all carry some vestige of it for our whole lives.

The problem for parents is that, as it concerns your children, you're not the hero anymore. The moment they are born *they* get to be the hero of their story and you take on a new role in their hero's journey. You are now the *guide*.

Every hero needs a guide. As the guide, we don't get the glory in the end because it's not our story. Mr. Miyagi doesn't kick Johnny in the face and hold up the trophy; Daniel LaRusso does. Morpheus doesn't rise from the dead and hack the Matrix; Neo does. Heck, Obi-Wan Kenobi and Yoda don't even live to see the Empire fall.

It's their story. You're just the guide . . . but that's not to say you still don't have an invaluable job. There is no hero, after all, without the guide.

Your new role is simple: Empower and equip the hero.

In the WHOLE Parent Method, once your kid is regulated,

it's time to empower and equip them for the long haul. There are a lot of ways to do this, but I'm going to give you three that I think work exceptionally well based on my experience and the best available research.

Empower Through Collaborative Problem Solving

I talked about this in chapter 4, but collaborative consequences are a great example of collaborative problem solving. Collaborative problem solving doesn't always have to be about consequences, though. Often, it's just that: problem solving.

If the issue is, for example, getting out of the house in the morning on time, ask your child what they think some good strategies might be. Younger children usually need to pick between options you provide, while older grade schoolers, preteens, and teenagers will be able to come up with solutions totally on their own. When they do, even if the ideas aren't what you would have come up with, celebrate it. It's a snapshot into their future when you won't be around and they will be left to parent themselves. They're building neural pathways in these moments that will serve them for the rest of their lives.

Celebration is not enough, though. The key to all of this is that you have to be willing to actually *consider* what they propose.

This is not the meaningless choice you give a toddler between putting the left or right shoe on first (though that is effective in its own way, especially when they're seeking autonomy). This is truly gaining their input because it is valuable to them and you, their guide. Just like with the collaborative consequences, they have insight into their own minds that you can't have. If they say listening to Rage Against the Machine as their alarm clock is going to get them up (as I did when this was my struggle at sixteen), trust them. If it doesn't work you can always reassess.

This is the ultimate power of the win-win mindset in action. When your kids know that you're seeking their flourishing on their terms, that you're ultimately preparing them to be in charge and the hero of their own story, they're going to help you do the work of discipline.

A simple way to do this is to sit down with your child around a problem when everyone is regulated (and you've gone through steps one through four in the Method) with a pen and a piece of paper and physically write out the solutions. When your child sees you writing their solutions out, physically putting them down on paper, it will communicate to them that you are involving them in the problem-solving process. If you feel you need to add a few potential solutions, you can offer those as well. (Pro tip here: Make sure at least one or two solutions you write have inherent flaws. You'll see why in a second.)

Write down all of their solutions, and—here is the most important point—you absolutely do not want to start criticizing or judging these potential solutions until you have all of them down on paper. If you do this it will backfire, undermining your child's sense of agency and reinforcing that you are ultimately uninterested in their collaboration. As a result, the solutions you come to will never be as effective.

One reason you *want* their input is to leverage and exercise their capacity for what researchers call *divergent thinking*.[1] Divergent thinking, for our purposes, can be classified as essentially creative problem solving or coming up with new ideas. Convergent thinking, processed in a different part of the brain, is our decision engine, logically considering the plausibility or efficacy of solutions.

The overwhelming majority of adults have developed (or have been conditioned, depending on which social neuroscientist you ask) to simultaneously use their *convergent* thinking to critique and shoot down their own *divergent* thinking as creative ideas occur. This means most of our best creative ideas never even make it to our conscious awareness.

Your kids, regardless of age, likely still have a higher capacity for creative problem solving and divergent thinking, as well as more information about what is causing the issue for them in the first place. So their ideas, even if they seem strange to you, actually have a much higher likelihood of being effective at solving the problem than you think.

Once they're all down on paper, you can talk about the potential issues with them, including those solutions you offered, highlighting what you like or dislike about them. If your kids are older they might say something like, "That one isn't going to work for me; it's not motivating." Bite your tongue. They're the hero and they are ultimately the one who will suffer the consequences if the solutions fail.

Eventually, you'll come up with a collaborative solution they can get behind that doesn't undermine the boundaries put in place for their safety and well-being and the safety of others. Win-win.

Empower Through Mistake Review

In Mistake Review, parents act as a consultant or coach revisiting a previous interaction or situation to determine together what went wrong and how it might be prevented in the future. If this sounds a lot like collaborative problem solving, that's because it is. Most of these ways of empowering and equipping your kids for the future are going to be various shades of the same.

What differentiates Mistake Review is that it centers the *problem* rather than the solution. That might seem counterproductive, but it's sometimes necessary.

As any serious professional athlete or even elite high school and college athlete will tell you, film is an important part of training and improvement. "Film" refers to the time spent with the coach or coaches slowly going through a previous practice or game and looking for where plays broke down or mistakes occurred.

Oftentimes even these high-level athletes, many of whom will go on to be highly successful coaches themselves, get caught up in the moment and make a mistake they're not even aware of. By methodically going through and picking apart the errors and mistakes with their coaches, the players learn how to adapt and train to not make those same mistakes again.

When I played volleyball at the Division II collegiate level, I both loved and hated film. Film without question makes you better at the game you're playing (even if you're watching film of other players), but it's also an incredibly vulnerable experience for someone who grew up with a fixed mindset. Every time I made a mistake that was subsequently slowed down to one-quarter speed and picked apart by a room full of coaches and teammates, I felt ashamed.

This is why it's massively important that you approach Mistake Review with a growth mindset. Growth mindset, as you'll remember, is the framework that assumes all of us are works in progress. Intelligence, aptitude, or athletic prowess in a growth mindset are things that are always changing and growing. People can get better and smarter. We're not stuck.

Fixed mindset, on the other hand, maintains that we are ultimately all bound by our natural abilities. Some people are smart, some are not. Some people are charismatic or good at piano, some are not. Some people are good at defense in volleyball, some are setters (a few of you will get that joke).

While you don't have the benefit of a perpetual recording of your child's life, you can still sit with them and talk about what happened and where it went wrong.

"Did you notice how upset your brother was about you playing with his toy? What can we do next time to try to prevent it from becoming a blowup?"

"You were really disappointed about not getting ice cream earlier. Can you tell me about that?"

Sometimes kids will get emotional just talking about and remembering the hard thing. That's OK! Just go through the Method again from step one: Consider the Wiring. Being a kid is hard, and sometimes so is being their guide.

Empower Through Improv ("Yes/And" and Role Reversal)

Another powerful tool our children possess is their imagination. It's for this reason that kids tend to get more scared of monsters than adults do, or create elaborate fictions to explain seemingly ordinary things.

As I mentioned in "Collaborative Problem Solving," their

imagination also allows them to problem-solve circles around your boring adult brain. For example, when your kids are scared of the aforementioned monsters, they actually have the ability, because of their imagination, to make themselves *less scared.*

Parents often foolishly try to apply logic in such situations. "There's no such thing as living skeletons. They couldn't exist! Stop worrying about it." It's an appeal to their *convergent* (judgment) thinking for a problem that originated in their *divergent* (imaginative) thinking.

Instead it would be better to appeal to their divergent thinking. We might say, "How can we imagine the skeleton in a way that makes him not scary and actually really silly?" And the response might be, "Put him on roller skates, and every time he falls down he becomes a pile of bones that dogs come and carry away to bury in the yard!"

Using the same principle, we can use their imagination to do all sorts of wonderful things that empower and equip them for lifelong flourishing. I'm going to give you two ways to do this.

First, we can anticipate future moral or relational dilemmas and cast ourselves in roles to play them out.

"What would you do if someone at school—let's call her Mary—told you that she stole the teacher's phone?" Or, "How would you respond if your friend Marcus told you he didn't want to be your friend anymore?"

Kids tend to love these exercises insofar as you engage with enthusiasm and they feel the freedom to problem-solve without judgment or repercussions. I call this being a nonjudgmental "Yes/And" participant with them.

In the theater art of improvisation there is a fundamental

rule that you cannot deny the reality another person onstage has created. If they say, "Your belt was magically turned into a poisonous snake," you go with it and respond accordingly. To say, "No it wasn't" kills the imaginative/creative process.

So too when you practice dilemmas with your kid. Even if they respond in a way you wish they wouldn't, like, "I wouldn't tell the teacher because I don't want Mary to get in trouble," or "I would punch Marcus right in the nose," just go with it.

"What do you think would happen if you did that? How would you feel? How would Marcus or the teacher feel?"

The resulting conversation actually prepares them to think more critically about their life, consider perspectives beyond their own, and become adults who make thoughtful ethical decisions.

A second way to apply this principle to past circumstances or events that are likely to happen in the immediate future is "role reversal."

In role reversal, the parent and child consent to take on each other's roles (or sometimes the child may take on the role of a different adult) in order to consider the situation from another's point of view. This is not just an abstract thought experiment; it's a dramatic enactment of the problematic situation.

As the scene plays out, oftentimes the child will correct the parent when the parent acts out of alignment with the child's actual perspective, granting both the parent and the child a window into the emotions underneath the surface. The child will also oftentimes tell the parent (who is playing the role of the child) exactly what they *need* to hear from an adult. Part of why this works is because, by removing themselves from the emotional stakes of the situation and taking on a different perspective, the child reengages their prefrontal cortex, allowing them to gain access to the logical part of their brain to assess the situation more clearly.

I can't tell you how many parents who were skeptical of role reversal begrudgingly tried it and came back to me later just blown away by its effectiveness. It really is amazing and works by combining many of the brain-based principles we've talked about in this book.

I recommend you try all of these different empowerment techniques in one form or another with your kids. Like the tools I offered in "Lead Them Out," each of these different ways of equipping your little hero is dependent on your child's development and temperament. As your child changes and grows, collaborative problem solving (something that can be a little beyond the development of toddlers) might become your new best friend. Others, like role reversal, that work fantastically with many younger kids, don't always work with preteens and teens (who might find the practice a little too silly). The key is to embrace your new role as their guide and just try. There is no one *right* way to raise resilient kids. Every kid is different and, even if it doesn't always feel like it, you are the expert on your kid.

Conclusion

I want to share three last things as you take what you've learned here and apply it to your life as a newly minted punishment-free parent. These are encouragements and affirmations that you can take and apply whether you choose to embody the things I've outlined in this book or not. Truly my hope for you is that you don't put this book down and feel like you're a worse parent than you initially thought.

That said, I've certainly been there. I've read hundreds of parenting books both in the process of writing this one and just generally for me. On my journey to parenting better, I have often felt like each "new method" or "new paradigm" just further exposes my flaws and inadequacies. There is a part of me that believes if those authors, the parenting experts of the world, ever met me in a Target and saw how I was parenting, they would be disgusted.

I know how incredibly overwhelming and defeating it can feel to learn how we *could* be doing better, especially for us parents who deeply and profoundly love our kids and care a ton about doing this right.

So here are the three things:

First, I want you to know that I honestly think you're rocking this whole parenting thing, even though you're not perfect. I truly mean that. I don't know you personally, but you're reading the conclusion of an emotionally and intellectually challenging parenting book. That means that you care enough to give this parenting thing your best shot—and as I've said to countless parents, your best is more than enough. But the fact that you read this book is not the only reason why I know you're the right person to be raising your kids. I know you're the right one for this job precisely because *you're their parent.* That incredible responsibility and burden also positions each and every one of us to have incredible, almost unparalleled influence. Parenting is the most rewarding, most challenging, and most important thing that any of us will ever do, all at once.

And it doesn't matter that you're not perfect. In fact, if you play your cards right, the moments when you're not can become the best parenting moments of all. Remember, growth mindset—the ability to learn from your mistakes rather than drown in them—is not only for your kids. It's for you too.

Second, when it gets hard, remember why you're choosing to parent differently. It's easy to get so caught up in the what and how of parenting that we forget the *why.* You're not parenting this way so that you can get your kids to put their shoes on and get out the door in less than half an hour and without screaming (although it's a nice perk). You're parenting this way because you're raising a full human who will live a whole, full, human life.

That means when you treat your kids with respect and

kindness, when you value growth over obedience and learning over punishment, when you hold them as they experience their big feelings rather than shaming or distracting them out of those feelings, when you model and hold boundaries, and when you walk them through the WHOLE Parent Method at age two, twelve, or seventeen . . . it doesn't really matter whether it's "working" that day to get them to do what they need to do. What matters is that you are setting them up for lifelong emotional, mental, physical, and relational health.

Third, when all else fails, give *yourself* advice. The single most difficult thing about parenting, more even than rewiring our brains out of our factory default settings, is self-doubt. Going home from the hospital you can't help but think, "Um, what am I supposed to do now?" It can feel like everyone else knows what they're doing, but you just didn't get the manual. Take it from a father of three who helps people all over the world do this parenting thing: The parenting experts don't feel like they know any more than you do.

I'll say it one more time for the cheap seats: The picture of parenting you see on social media is not real. Every single one of us, no matter how confident we sound in sound bites or in quippy little videos, feels exactly the same way sometimes.

It can feel like you just don't know what to do or where to turn. In those moments I hope you think to pick up this book and flip it open. But before you do, grab a piece of paper and a pen and imagine that it's not you who needs the parenting advice. Do a little role reversal. Imagine your friend, who has a kid or kids the same age as yours and shares your values, is experiencing this problem. Then write them a letter.

Give them the advice I know you already have buried deep down inside of you. Empathize with them and validate that everyone struggles with kids sometimes. Tell them what you've learned from your years on this earth and the books you've read. Tell them how the experiences you've had with your kids apply to their situation. Give them step by step what you think they should do and encourage them to stick to it. Then, when you've finished the letter, read it as if someone else wrote it to you.

In that letter is contained all the parenting wisdom you need to be the best version of yourself for you and your kids.

And so, finally, I leave you with this:

You are worthy of love, belonging, dignity, and respect. You don't have to earn any of it. Neither do your children. I wish you all the best, my friend. Good luck.

Acknowledgments

I am incredibly grateful to all those who have helped me on my own parenting journey as well as on the journey to the publication of *Punishment-Free Parenting*. The life lessons and encouragement I have received from colleagues, mentors, friends, and family are overwhelming. Specifically, I want to thank a few people by name.

First, to my wife, Jess, it's hard to put into words how invaluable you have been in this process. From handing me my first parenting book (and then getting on me when I didn't actually read it) to supporting me through writing my *own* first parenting book, I could not do this without you. You outlined the book with me more than once. You read it when it was a mess and didn't say it was. You watched the kids for far more than your share of the time while I sat at the computer putting words on a page. You even led me through the process of getting a title, subtitle, and cover. Most of all, you inspire me to be a better parent every single day. This is yours as much as it is mine.

To my own parents, Karla and Steve, I couldn't have written this book about breaking cycles if you hadn't broken cycles yourselves. The most important lesson you taught me was to absolutely love being a parent. You both modeled that for me. Even though parenting brings with it some of the hardest moments in the world, you showed me that being a parent also gave you the best moments. Above all else, I have never doubted once that you loved me with your whole hearts.

To my in-laws, Dave and Linda, you were the first grown-ups I knew who thought brains were cool and worth studying. Watching how you have loved our kids has brought me so much joy. Thank you especially for trusting me and Jess to figure out parenting and following our lead with the kids. So many adults spend so much time and effort trying to make their parents proud. Thanks for making it clear that I didn't need to worry about that.

To those who have been an integral part of this book as processing partners and editors, I am in your debt forever. Again, that includes my wife, Jess, and also two of my best friends Eli Harwood and Cheryl Lynn Cain; my agent/informal therapist, Kathleen Kerr; my friend Jenny, who shared the burden of caring so well for my kids while I wrote; and my editor, Matthew Burdette, and all those at Convergent who took a shot on me and worked on this project.

To all my mentors and colleagues in the parenting space who have encouraged me, I am grateful for you more than you know. To Dan Siegel, who, along with Tina Payne Bryson, wrote my favorite parenting books. And to Tina, especially. You were and are my personal parenting hero. When I wasn't sure if this book was any good, you assured me it was before you ever read it. It was beyond my wildest dreams that you would write the foreword for my first book, and, in spite of all you had going on, you made that dream come true. I will never be able to thank you enough for what you've given me as a dad and now as an author. To Aliza, who hosts my favorite podcast. And to the countless others who have written the parenting books that have gotten me to where I am today: Thank you. Many of you I will likely never meet, but you laid the groundwork for *Punishment-Free Parenting*. And especially to those of you whom I also get to call friends, I am the better for your place in my life.

To all those who have joined the Whole Parent Membership, and especially those of you who regularly show up at virtual group coaching and workshops, this book is a direct byproduct of your trusting me to help you parent better.

To the rest of the Whole Parent community, whether you joined the email list, subscribed to the podcast, followed me on social media (especially in the early days), or have ever simply liked, shared, or commented on a video, I didn't know how many other parents needed this stuff until you showed me and encouraged me. A special thank you to Nina Wolfensberger, the Instagram follower who inspired the subtitle for this book by replying to a post.

And finally to you, the reader of this book: To you I am as grateful as almost anyone else. My goal is to make the world a better place by helping parents to raise the next generation. You read my book and are helping me do just that (especially if you pass it on to a friend).

Notes

Chapter 1: The Problem with Punishment

1. J. Durrant and R. Ensom, "Physical Punishment of Children: Lessons from 20 Years of Research," *Canadian Medical Association Journal* 184(12) (Sept. 4, 2012):1373–77; doi: 10.1503/cmaj.101314.
2. Tom W. Smith, Michael Hout, and Peter V. Marsden, "General Social Survey, 1972–2012" [Cumulative File] Codebook, ICPSR 34802, Inter-University Consortium for Political and Social Research (ICPSR), people.wku.edu/douglas.smith/GSS%201972_2012%20Codebook.pdf.
3. Ibid.
4. Ibid.
5. End Corporal Punishment, 2018, endcorporalpunishment.org/countdown.
6. Durrant and Ensom, "Physical Punishment of Children."
7. J. Bart Klika, Julia M. Fleckman, and Melissa T. Merrick, "Physical Punishment: Attitudes, Behaviors, and Norms Associated with Its Use Across the U.S.," Prevent Child Abuse America, 2021, preventchildabuse.org/wp-content/uploads/2021/05/

Prevent-Child-Abuse-America-2021-Physical-Punishment
-Report.pdf.

8. Naomi I. Eisenberger, Matthew D. Lieberman, and Kipling D. Williams, "Does Rejection Hurt? An fMRI Study of Social Exclusion," *Science* 302(5643) (2003): 290–92; doi.org/10.1126/science.1089134.

9. Ibid.

10. "Understanding the Stress Response," Harvard Health Publishing, Apr. 3, 2024, health.harvard.edu/staying-healthy/understanding-the-stress-response.

11. Ethan Kross et al., "Social Rejection Shares Somatosensory Representations with Physical Pain," *PNAS* 108(15) (March 2011): 6270–75; doi.org/10.1073/pnas.1102693108.

12. Daniel S. Nagin, "Deterrence in the Twenty-First Century," *Crime and Justice* 42(1) (2013): 201–2; doi.org/10.1086/670398.

13. "Pathways Between Child Maltreatment and Adult Criminal Involvement," National Institute of Justice, Oct. 11, 2017, nij.ojp.gov/topics/articles/pathways-between-child-maltreatment-and-adult-criminal-involvement.

Chapter 2: Get Curious, Not Furious

1. Abraham Maslow, "A Theory of Human Motivation," *Psychological Review* 50(4) (1943): 370–96; doi.org/10.1037/h0054346.

2. Louis Cozolino, *The Pocket Guide to Neuroscience for Clinicians* (New York: Norton, 2020).

3. Suzanna Herculano-Houzel, "The Human Brain in Numbers: A Linearly Scaled-Up Primate Brain," *Frontiers in Human Neuroscience* 3 (2009); doi.org/10.3389/neuro.09.031.2009.

4. Ibid.

5. D. Schwartz and L. J. Proctor, "Community Violence Exposure and Children's Social Adjustment in the School Peer Group: The Mediating Roles of Emotion Regulation and Social Cognition," *Journal of Consulting and Clinical Psychology* 68(4) (2000): 670–83; doi.org/10.1037/0022-006X.68.4.670.

Chapter 3: What Is Modeled Is Mirrored

1. Moira Burke, Justin Cheng, and Bethany de Gant, "Social Comparison and Facebook: Feedback, Positivity, and Opportunities for Comparison," *CHI '20: Proceedings of the 2020 CHI Conference on Human Factors in Computing Systems* (April 2020), 1–13; dl.acm.org/doi/10.1145/3313831.3376482#sec-cit.

2. Brené Brown, *The Gifts of Imperfection* (Minneapolis: Hazelden Information & Educational Services, 2010).

3. K. Limburg, H. J. Watson, M. S. Hagger, and S. J. Egan, "The Relationship Between Perfectionism and Psychopathology: A Meta-Analysis," *Journal of Clinical Psychology* 73 (2017): 1301–26; doi.org/10.1002/jclp.22435.

4. Thomas Curran, Andrew P. Hill, and Luke J. Williams, "The Relationships Between Parental Conditional Regard and Adolescents' Self-Critical and Narcissistic Perfectionism," *Personality and Individual Differences* 109(1) (Dec. 2016): 17–22; researchgate.net/publication/311717373_The_relationships_between_parental_conditional_regard_and_adolescents%27_self-critical_and_narcissistic_perfectionism.

5. M. M. Smith, S. B. Sherry, S. Chen et al., "The Perniciousness of Perfectionism: A Meta-Analytic Review of the Perfectionism–Suicide Relationship," *Journal of Personality* 86(3) (2018): 522–42; doi.org/10.1111/jopy.12333.

6. Albert Bandura, Dorothea Ross, and Sheila A. Ross, "Transmission of Aggression Through Imitation of Aggressive Models," *Journal of Abnormal and Social Psychology* 63(3) (1961): 575–82; doi.org/10.1037/h0045925.

7. Richard P. Cooper et al., "Associative (Not Hebbian) Learning and the Mirror Neuron System," *Neuroscience Letters* 540(X) (April 2013): 28–36; doi.org/10.1016/j.neulet.2012.10.002.

8. Roderik J. S. Gerritsen and Guido P. H. Band, "Breath of Life: The Respiratory Vagal Stimulation Model of Contemplative Activity," *Frontiers in Human Neuroscience* 12 (2018); frontiersin.org/articles/10.3389/fnhum.2018.00397/full?fbclid=IwAR3oR

ry6iexWHx0yJubJt0HFcA6ESlPulL73yEmA4YwcbR2UUy 2XraTCmvg.

Chapter 4: Using Consequence Effectively

1. Matthew Hays, Nate Kornell, and Robert Bjork, "The Costs and Benefits of Providing Feedback During Learning," *Psychonomic Bulletin & Review* 17(6) (2010): 797–801. doi.org/10.3758/PBR.17.6.797. See also Harold Pashler et al., "When Does Feedback Facilitate Learning of Words?" *Journal of Experimental Psychology: Learning, Memory and Cognition* 31(1) (January 2005): 3–8; doi.org/0.1037/0278-7393.31.1.3.

2. Manu Kapur, "Examining Productive Failure, Productive Success, Unproductive Failure, and Unproductive Success in Learning," *Educational Psychologist* 51(2) (2016): 289–99; doi.org/10.1080/00461520.2016.1155457.

3. L. E. Richland, N. Kornell, and L. S. Kao, "The Pretesting Effect: Do Unsuccessful Retrieval Attempts Enhance Learning?" *Journal of Experimental Psychology: Applied* 15(3) (Sept. 2009): 243–57; doi.org/10.1037/a0016496.

4. Dr. Aliza Pressman, *The 5 Principles of Parenting: Your Essential Guide to Raising Good Humans* (New York: Simon & Schuster, 2024), 181.

5. Michaeleen Doucleff, "'Anti-Dopamine Parenting' Can Curb a Kid's Craving for Screens or Sweets," NPR, June 12, 2023, npr.org/sections/health-shots/2023/06/12/1180867083/tips-to-outsmart-dopamine-unhook-kids-from-screens-sweets.

Chapter 5: Boundaries

1. Jonathan Haidt, *The Anxious Generation: How the Great Rewiring of Childhood Is Causing an Epidemic of Mental Illness* (New York: Penguin Press, 2024).

2. "Sports Injury Statistics," Stanford Medicine: Children's Health website, accessed Dec. 12, 2023, stanfordchildrens.org/en/topic/default?id=sports-injury-statistics-90-P02787.

3. Harumi Ito and Darin Lee, "Assessing the Impact of the September 11 Terrorist Attacks on U.S. Airline Demand," *Journal of*

Economics and Business 57(1) (Jan.–Feb. 2005): 75–95; doi.org/ 10.1016/j.jeconbus.2004.06.003.

4. *Stereotypical kidnapping* is defined as "A nonfamily abduction in which a slight acquaintance or stranger moves a child (age 0–17) at least twenty feet or holds the child at least one hour, and in which one or more of the following circumstances occurs: The child is detained overnight, transported at least fifty miles, held for ransom, abducted with intent to keep the child permanently, or killed," unh.edu/ccrc/sites/default/files/media/ 2022-02/child-victims-of-stereotypical-kidnappings-known-to -law-enforcement-in-2011.pdf.

5. Ibid. See also Lenore Skenazy, "A Parent's Nightmare— Increasingly Unlikely," *Wall Street Journal,* June 20, 2016, wsj .com/articles/a-parents-nightmareincreasingly-unlikely -1466465122.

6. Warwick Cairns, *How to Live Dangerously: The Hazards of Helmets, the Benefits of Bacteria, and the Risks of Living Too Safe* (New York: St. Martin's Griffin, 2009), 45.

7. CDC Youth Risk Behavior Survey: Data Summary and Trends Report 2011–2021, Page 2, cdc.gov/healthyyouth/data/yrbs/pdf/ YRBS_Data-Summary-Trends_Report2023_508.pdf.

8. Steven Berkowitz, "The Youth Mental Health Crisis Worsens amid a Shortage of Professional Help Providers," *Scientific American*, Aug. 18, 2023, scientificamerican.com/article/the -youth-mental-health-crisis-worsens-amid-a-shortage-of -professional-help-providers. See also Alicia VanOrman and Beth Jarosz, "Suicide Replaces Homicide as Second-Leading Cause of Death Among U.S. Teenagers," Population Reference Bureau website, June 9, 2016, prb.org/resources/suicide -replaces-homicide-as-second-leading-cause-of-death-among -u-s-teenagers.

9. Haidt, *Anxious Generation*.

10. Ibid.

11. Kristy Benoit Allen et al., "Parental Autonomy Granting and Child Perceived Control: Effects on the Everyday Emotional Experience of Anxious Youth," *Journal of Child Psychology and*

Psychiatry 57(7) (July 2016): 835–42; doi.org/10.1111/jcpp
.12482.

Chapter 6: Unleashing Our Emotional Superpowers

1. Daniel Goleman, "Can Emotional Intelligence Be Learned?"
   YouTube, March 8, 2018, youtube.com/watch?v=sfT55
   TZV-20.
2. Brené Brown, *Atlas of the Heart* (New York: Random House,
   2021), xxi.
3. Mary Mills West, *Infant Care* (Washington, D.C.: U.S. Government Printing Office, 1914), 60–61. https://www.mchlibrary
   .org/history/chbu/3121-1914.PDF
4. John B. Watson, *Psychological Care of Infant and Child* (New
   York: W. W. Norton & Company, 1928), 81–82.
5. James Watson, quoted in Corrine Smirle, "Profile: Rosalie
   Rayner," *Feminist Voices* blog, 2013, feministvoices.com/
   profiles/rosalie-rayner.
6. Therese Oneill, "'Don't Think of Ugly People': How Parenting
   Advice Has Changed," *The Atlantic*, Apr. 19, 2013, theatlantic
   .com/health/archive/2013/04/dont-think-of-ugly-people-how
   -parenting-advice-has-changed/275108/.
7. Kristin Kobes Du Mez, *Jesus and John Wayne: How White Evan-
   gelicals Corrupted a Faith and Fractured a Nation* (New York:
   Liveright, 2020), 79.
8. Marc Brackett, "Become an Emotion Scientist in 2020," Marc
   Brackett blog, Jan. 5, 2020, marcbrackett.com/become-an
   -emotion-scientist-in-2020.

Chapter 7: Becoming Conscious

1. Gabor Maté, *The Myth of Normal: Trauma, Illness, and Healing
   in a Toxic Culture* (New York: Avery, 2022), 20.
2. Jeremy Shapiro, "Two Parts of the Brain Govern Much of Mental Life," *Psychology Today*, Nov. 5, 2021, psychologytoday.com/
   us/blog/thinking-in-black-white-and-gray/202111/two-parts-the
   -brain-govern-much-mental-life.
3. "Traumatic vs. Sad Memories: How PTSD Alters Brain Func-

tion," *SciTechDaily*, Nov. 30, 2023, www.scitechdaily.com/
traumatic-vs-sad-memories-how-ptsd-alters-brain-function.

4. Judith Herman, M.D., *Trauma and Recovery: The Aftermath of Violence—from Domestic Abuse to Political Terror* (New York: Basic Books, 2022).

5. Shefali Tsabary, *The Conscious Parent: Transforming Ourselves, Empowering Our Children* (Vancouver, BC: Namaste Publishing, 2010), 23.

6. Bruce McEwan, "When Is Stress Good for You?" *Aeon*, July 11, 2017, aeon.co/essays/how-stress-works-in-the-human-body-to-make-or-break-us.

7. Herman, *Trauma and Recovery*.

Chapter 8: Repair and Reconciliation

1. Jonathan Haidt, *The Anxious Generation: How the Great Rewiring of Childhood Is Causing an Epidemic of Mental Illness* (New York: Penguin Press, 2024).

2. E. Z. Tronick, "Emotions and Emotional Communication in Infants," *American Psychologist* 44(2) (1989): 112–19; doi.org/10.1037/0003-066X.44.2.112.

3. Dr. Aliza Pressman, *The 5 Principles of Parenting: Your Essential Guide to Raising Good Humans* (New York: Simon & Schuster, 2024).

Chapter 9: Consider the Wiring

1. Mind and Life Education Research Network (MLERN), "Contemplative Practices and Mental Training: Prospects for American Education," Child Development Perspectives 6(2) (June 2012):146–53; doi.org/10.1111/j.1750-8606.2012.00240.x.

Chapter 10: Honor the Experience

1. Katelyn Gomes, "There's a Reason Why You Want That Hug: The Science and Importance of Physical Contact," Mind Beacon, n.d., mindbeacon.com/strongerminds/the-science-and-importance-of-physical-contact.

2. Aliza Pressman, "5 Ways to Support Toddlers' Big Feelings,"

Raising Good Humans with Dr. Aliza Pressman, Substack, Sept. 27, 2023, dralizapressman.substack.com/p/5-ways-to -support-toddlers-big-feelings.

3. Daniel J. Siegel and Tina Payne Bryson, *The Whole Brain Child: 12 Revolutionary Strategies to Nurture Your Child's Developing Mind* (New York: Delacorte Press, 2012), 29.

Chapter 12: Lead Them Out

1. Stephen R. Covey, *The 7 Habits of Highly Effective People* (New York: Simon & Schuster, 2020), 238.

2. Ibid., 240.

3. JongEun Yim, "Therapeutic Benefits of Laughter in Mental Health: A Theoretical Review," *Tohoku J Exp Med.* 2016 Jul., 239(3):243–49. doi: 10.1620/tjem.239.243. PMID: 27439375.

4. Vesa Putkinen, Sanaz Nazari-Farsani, Kerttu Seppälä et al., "Decoding Music-Evoked Emotions in the Auditory and Motor Cortex," *Cerebral Cortex* 31(5) (May 2021): 2549–60; doi.org/ 10.1093/cercor/bhaa373.

Chapter 13: Empower for the Future

1. "Divergent Thinking," ScienceDirect, sciencedirect.com/topics/ psychology/divergent-thinking.

Index

___

About the Author

JON FOGEL is a husband, a father of four beautiful children, and a parenting educator. His goal is to teach how to parent more effectively—with less stress and more success. In his teaching, Fogel combines modern neuroscience, developmental psychology, counseling, and positive, "gentle parenting" wisdom, distilling the science into terms every parent can understand. He has worked in counseling environments for the past decade and specifically with thousands of parents in one-on-one and group settings to achieve incredible transformation in their parenting. Jon Fogel holds a master of divinity degree from North Park Theological Seminary.

About the Type

This book was set in Fairfield, the first typeface from the hand of the distinguished American artist and engraver Rudolph Ruzicka (1883–1978). Ruzicka was born in Bohemia (in the present-day Czech Republic) and came to America in 1894. He set up his own shop, devoted to wood engraving and printing, in New York in 1913 after a varied career working as a wood engraver, in photoengraving and banknote printing plants, and as an art director and freelance artist. He designed and illustrated many books, and was the creator of a considerable list of individual prints— wood engravings, line engravings on copper, and aquatints.